About the Author

Mary Lynn Mason is a child of divorced and absent parents. She has been taking care of herself and has had a job since she was fourteen. Mary is a mother of a bi-racial son and struggled as a single mom for many years doing whatever it took to take care of her child. She is not proud of some of the things she did, but survival was her only option. Along the way, she made terrible choices in love and those bad choices ended with her telling this story. She believes now the healing from those choices can finally begin.

Full Circle: Made for the Highway

Mary Lynn Mason

Full Circle: Made for the Highway

Olympia Publishers
London

www.olympiapublishers.com
OLYMPIA PAPERBACK EDITION

Copyright © Mary Lynn Mason 2024

The right of Mary Lynn Mason to be identified as author of
this work has been asserted in accordance with sections 77 and 78 of
the Copyright, Designs and Patents Act 1988.

All Rights Reserved

No reproduction, copy or transmission of this publication
may be made without written permission.
No paragraph of this publication may be reproduced,
copied or transmitted save with the written permission of the publisher,
or in accordance with the provisions
of the Copyright Act 1956 (as amended).

Any person who commits any unauthorized act in relation to
this publication may be liable to criminal
prosecution and civil claims for damage.

A CIP catalog record for this title is
available from the British Library.

ISBN: 978-1-83543-135-1

First Published in 2024

Olympia Publishers
Tallis House
2 Tallis Street
London
EC4Y 0AB

Printed in Great Britain

Dedication

I dedicate this book to my son; he is my reason for life, for love, for everything.

Acknowledgments

Thank you, Mom, for spending countless hours and many tears helping me edit this book and for your unconditional love and support throughout my life. Thank you to my father in Heaven for being my guiding light now even though you couldn't when you were alive. Thanks to my "truck driver" for giving me the ending to this story that I didn't see coming.

Introduction

It's a weekday in the middle of October 2022. After a few years of contemplating and not knowing the end of this story, I finally found the motivation to start writing a story about my life and where I am today.

This story is about my connection to the highway, road trips, love, toxic relationships, and how I became a flight attendant after being a drug mule. I believe wholeheartedly that it's only due to my white privilege that becoming a flight attendant was even possible after that.

White privilege is starting to be recognized, and this is my story to contribute to the proof of it. I hope to make people that are in denial regarding white privilege aware and bring that awareness by sharing this story.

This story is also about me having a connection to semi-trucks at a very young age. Now years later, and after much heartbreak, love is possible again and how my connection to semi-trucks led to that.

About seven months ago, I met a man on the plane with some Hollywood connections. We've texted occasionally over the past few months, but a few days ago we had a more in-depth conversation, also via text.

The conversation was mostly flirty, setting terms of our expectations for each other if we were going to date.

I've enjoyed texting with this man very much. There are no simple text messages. He sends paragraphs when most men send a word or two. I paid attention to the words he used and appreciated his writing skills and vocabulary.

Because of his experience as a professional writer and his obvious talent for writing, I decided to ask him if he would help me write this story.

I mentioned to him that I didn't think I had the skill to write or the vocabulary to do so. I told him I thought my story was profound, but putting these thoughts and memories of my life on paper, whether fiction or nonfiction, would be difficult. Sharing it with a virtual stranger would also be difficult, since that would put me in a vulnerable place that I wouldn't be comfortable with, but I desperately wanted his opinion on whether the story was good enough to publish. I figured my best approach would be to ask him if he would sign an NDA.

My interest in writing this story isn't necessarily for money, but I'm sure there is potential for a lot of money and since it is my story and my story alone, having someone take it out from under me was a concern.

I've shared parts of this story with family and friends over the years, but not with anyone or with enough detail that they could help me write or publish it.

My initial thought was to ask him to sign an NDA, tell the story to him, and let him write it. That didn't happen.

His response to me asking him to sign an NDA was simple: he didn't sign NDAs unless there was money up front. I didn't have that kind of savings or money to invest in this story so that went in one ear and out the other. I told him that the story was profound and that people involved could be exposed, that it was relevant to current social injustice in our country, but that even with the social relevance, it was also a heart-wrenching love story that women in abusive or toxic relationships could relate with. But that I didn't have the ending to my story, certainly not a happy one, so I didn't know where to begin.

He told me that I didn't need the "ending" to begin writing and that the "ending" would find me. That's the best advice anyone has ever given me regardless of this story. Speaking of profound, this was exactly what I needed to hear to start writing.

So, that is how I began...

October 2022
Present Day

I'm single. I love my life and my career as a flight attendant, but I do feel there's something missing, yet I haven't quite put my finger on it. Maybe it's the right man or a different career, but for the most part I'm happy.

It's seven a.m. at the beach. I live in a perfect studio apartment five minutes to where I park at the airport and one block from the ocean. My windows are open because I don't have air conditioning. The ocean air is enough to keep my apartment cool even in the summer, since most days the temperature doesn't rise above eighty. I can hear the ocean, but I can also hear the sound of the Teslas in the neighborhood hustling off to work. I love the sound of the ocean, but the sound of the Teslas is somehow annoying to me; maybe because I still drive a gas-guzzling Mercedes SUV.

It's a beautiful morning and I'm off work today. Not flying anywhere. I'm on reserve, which means on the days "on," I sit at home on call and wait to be called for a trip not knowing where I'd be flying. I have to be on reserve three times a year. The other nine months, I'm a line holder, so I know in advance where I'm flying the entire month. When I'm on reserve, my days off aren't so great; Monday and Tuesday.

I love my career and being a flight attendant is a blessing. Becoming a flight attendant was the beginning of stable income, job satisfaction without stress, and plenty of opportunity to meet men! It is the beginning of this story's "possible" happy ending.

June 2010
Second Time Arrested

Part 1

Believe it or not, I'm a flight attendant and not behind bars today because of white privilege. I gave a black man at least fifteen years of his life because of my white privilege...

It's late on a Thursday night, in early June 2010. I had been running like this about every two months for the last two years. I shouldn't have been driving this late, especially in a black Suburban with California plates. I was in Kansas on I-70. I should have been on a smaller back road and at midnight, I should have been in a hotel or taking a nap in a rest area, but I needed to keep going. I needed to get to my destination, not to deliver the product which I had to do anyway, but, instead, so that I could catch Marcus, my boyfriend, cheating. I didn't care about anything else, including how irresponsible all of that was.

My plan was to arrive eight to ten hours early and catch Marcus in the act. I knew he was cheating, but I wanted to see it for myself. I wanted these last two years of stress and anxiety to be over and catching him would be my easy way out. Instead, I was the one who got caught.

I think I subconsciously wanted to get caught since that would be easier than the hurt I would feel when I actually caught Marcus with another woman.

It was pitch black at midnight other than the still surprising amount of cars and semis on the highway. There was a diesel in front of me. I'll never forget the blue writing on the white Conway truck.

The driver was going under the speed limit. I decided to pass him on the left, as a good driver would do, but a few seconds later, I saw blue and red lights in my rear-view mirror. This wasn't the first time I had been pulled over, but this was the largest amount of marijuana I'd ever taken, and even though I never knew the exact amount, I could tell by the amount of space it was taking up in the large SUV I was driving. My nerves instantly went through the roof when I saw the lights. It didn't make sense to me at the time why I was being pulled over. I wasn't speeding, I used my blinker, etc. etc.

I know now I was pulled over because of the car I was driving that late at night. With no choice, I pulled to the side of the highway. I tried to compose myself and think of the best way to proceed. While the officer approached the vehicle, I sent a text message to Marcus saying that I got pulled over and the officer approaching was using his mag light shining it into the back of the vehicle.

My heart was racing, but in stressful situations I've always been able to remain calm or at least appear that way. It's what makes me a great flight attendant today.

I pressed the button that rolled my window down. I spoke first and said, "Hello, did I do something wrong?"

He said, "Yes, you passed that diesel too closely." I wasn't going to argue with the officer, but I had certainly not passed too close. Is that even a traffic violation? I know traffic laws. I started doing road trips alone when I was nineteen...

Childhood and Beyond
Made for the Highway

Ever since I was a little girl, I've been fascinated with semi-trucks. My aunt and uncle drove them together for many years. I remember climbing up in their truck when I was about eight. They drove it to our house to show my mom and dad without a trailer attached. I fell in love with their blue semi that day. But that's all I got to do—climb up and sit there. We didn't even go around the block, but I felt a connection to their truck that day. I remember thinking how happy my aunt and uncle looked as a couple, something I didn't see when I looked at my parents. I never saw my parents fight and they didn't hate each other, I just didn't see them "love" each other.

Later as an adult, I developed a fear of semis and a respect for their power when a family member of mine was killed on I-10 west of Phoenix. One semi driver had fallen asleep and hit my step-uncle from behind, pushing him into another semi, crushing his small truck and killing him instantly. As a child and young adult, I'd experienced losing a loved one, but that was due to old age, not a terrible accident.

To this day, when I'm on the highway, I never put myself in the position to be in between two semi-trucks.

I knew at a very young age I would be traveling on highways often. I even joked with friends and family that I was a truck driver in a past life.

1991
First Road Trip Alone

As a kid, we went on road trips a lot. I never even flew on an airplane until I was seventeen. Lots of people in the airline industry grew up around it but not me. We did a lot of camping and fishing trips all over Arizona and even some to California for summer vacations. But we always drove for our family vacations.

My first road trip alone was when I was nineteen. I followed my boyfriend, later husband, and father of my son from city to city to watch him play baseball.

I had just purchased a brand new 1991 Eclipse, and I couldn't wait to hit the road.

The first place I was scheduled to meet him was Colorado. I'd been a passenger in a car or truck many times driving through the mountains in Arizona but never the driver and never alone.

The drive up the I-17 to Flagstaff was beautiful, and it was summer so no snow or any weather issues. Once I got to Flagstaff, the highway over to New Mexico was I-40. The road from Flagstaff to Albuquerque is long and straight and flat.

My mom was always the "fast" driver out of my parents so I thought why not, girls can drive fast. I took my little Eclipse as fast as she could go. My Eclipse had a manual stick shift and every car I had as a teenager were also stick shifts, so I knew how to drive them well. The Eclipse was the last stick shift I owned but somehow, the muscle memory still exists in me.

Once I got in fifth gear, I pushed her to about 115 mph then the rpm got too high and I didn't have a sixth gear, so that was the max speed I could go. It felt good and I knew I'd always be a good fast driver after that, but I needed to slow my ass down.

It's a good thing I did because about ten miles down the road there were police everywhere, and an actual road block. There weren't many cars on the road, and I could see the roadblock in the distance. I stopped at the roadblock and rolled down my window. This was my first encounter, being in a vehicle as the driver and being questioned by an officer.

He asked where I was going and that was it. I had no clue what they were looking for, but it wasn't me. This was many years prior to my drug mule days so I didn't have anything illegal in my car, and I went on my merry way.

I stopped somewhere in New Mexico because as a brand-new road trip driver there was no way I was making it all the way to Colorado from Phoenix in one day. I didn't have a cell phone or GPS. I had to communicate with my mom and James, my boyfriend, from a pay phone, and I had to use actual paper maps to navigate my trip.

The next day I didn't have as much luck with the weather. I made it to northern New Mexico, and almost to Colorado, when I ran into a horrific hail storm. This was my first, but certainly not the last, road trip driving through a horrible storm. I was nervous about the storm but pushed through it.

Instinctively, I paid attention to what the semi drivers were doing, put my hazard lights on, drove slowly and prayed for the best. The storm lasted longer than I prayed for, but I got to my destination in Colorado safe and sound.

My brand-new Eclipse had a little hail damage on the roof, three deep dents, but that was it. I gained essential bad weather road trip knowledge, that I became grateful for years later.

June 2010
Second Time Arrested

Part 2

Back on the side of the road in Kansas and in the black Chevy Suburban, that I rented from Dollar Rent a Car at an airport in Arizona, the officer asked for my license and registration. I gave it to him. He then asked for permission to search my vehicle and I told him no, I told him that I had to use the restroom, that I needed to pee badly, and that I wanted to do that first. Yes, I needed to pee, but what I really needed was more time.

Crazy as it sounds, this officer decided to let me drive to the next exit and go to the gas station. I couldn't believe it, but my plan to buy time worked.

He followed me in his SUV cruiser to the exit. When I got out of my black SUV to use the restroom, I was praying that was going to be the end of it, and he was going to let me go.

Before I got out of the SUV, I stuffed my cell phone in my pants and only had my keys in my hand as I exited.

I exited the vehicle, but the officer forced me to leave my keys behind. That was the only way he was going to allow me to go into the gas station to use the restroom. I didn't have a choice. Arguing with the officer wasn't going to get me anywhere, and all I could think about was getting to the bathroom so I could text Marcus what was happening.

I'll never forget the look on the gas station attendant's face. His eye balls were popping out. I can only imagine what he was thinking, as he saw my SUV pull in, because there was a cop behind me with his lights on.

I walked past the attendant, without saying a word, and went into the restroom. The officer took my keys, but I didn't have anything else in my hands so he didn't know I had my phone or he didn't care. I quickly texted Marcus again, telling him that I was in a gas station bathroom now and that my SUV was most likely going to be searched. I'm sure this sounded unbelievable to him at the time. It still does to me now as I write this. There was no time for me to wait for him to respond, and I didn't know if he even would. As soon as I came out from the restroom and walked back outside, the officer had his handcuffs out and told me that I was going to be arrested. The officer searched my SUV without my permission while I was in the restroom and he found the weed.

He immediately handcuffed me and put me in his vehicle in the back seat and drove me to a shed somewhere a few miles off of the highway.

That short ride was a blur, but he must have read me my rights while he was handcuffing me.

This officer asked me questions for quite some time while another officer, also a highway patrol, joined him after he brought my SUV to the site where they were questioning me.

I was just sitting there at a table in what looked like a garage of some kind, not a police station. I'd been in a shed similar to this when I was arrested several months prior. They did remove the handcuffs, but there were three officers now and it was dark outside. I didn't know where I was and clearly wasn't going to try to run away from them.

They asked me random questions and searched the vehicle again apparently with more detail this time. They had some sort of scale, and they determined that I had 364 lbs. of marijuana in my car!

I heard them whispering to each other that this amount was too much for them to process locally and that the DEA would have to come investigate. I can't explain or even put into words what I was going through at that moment.

I consider myself to be an honest person, but in those moments I needed to say everything I could to save myself and Marcus. An hour went by with me just sitting there waiting to see what was going to happen next.

The DEA officers arrived about two hours after I originally arrived at the shed. The two DEA officers started asking me questions, like where I got the weed, who gave it to me, where I was taking it, and how I got myself into this situation.

I was very vague. I knew my right not to speak at all. I told them that I didn't know the answer to any of their questions, that it was the first time I had done this, and that all I did was open my garage back home. Then someone loaded the weed in the rented SUV and I got on the road the next day heading east.

I told them I didn't know where I was going. I didn't have and wasn't given a final destination, and that the person I was going to meet was supposed to call me and tell me where to go once I got close to their destination and far enough east.

None of that was true. I gave as little info as possible to protect myself and Marcus on the other end.

Because I was on I-70, I quickly did the navigation in my head and came up with a story to tell the DEA. I told them that I was going to Virginia. Virginia wasn't my destination but a state near that. Virginia made sense to them, since where they caught me and where they were interrogating me was due west of Virginia.

At the beginning of the interrogation, one of the male officers searched me. All of the officers including the DEA were male. You would think that a female officer should have been the one to search me but that didn't happen and at the time I didn't care.

I was extremely uncomfortable sitting in this shed/garage with now five male officers, but the actual pat down / search didn't scare me. I was more worried about being physically harmed or sexually assaulted by one or all of these men. I was also worried about what they would find on my phone. I wondered if, somehow, they would be able to recover everything that I just deleted, and worrying about that helped take my mind of the fact that I had no clue where I was, no one that loved or cared about me knew where I was, and I was in the middle of nowhere in a shed surrounded by five men with guns.

I was smart back at the gas station. Not one text to Marcus would show since I deleted all of our messages to each other. I even deleted him as a contact. I still figured that law enforcement would have some kind of technology to retrieve what I deleted, but that didn't happen.

The DEA officers went through my phone and used pictures of my son as their ammunition.

After hours of questioning and threatening, telling me that the cartel was going to come after me and my son, the sun was coming up. Prior to that moment I never even considered that who Marcus was dealing with was the "cartel."

The DEA knew they were not getting anywhere with me, so instead they asked me to continue my journey in my same rented black SUV with the weed in tow and they would follow me close behind.

They said they would arrest the people that I dropped the weed off to then let me go with no charges. Go fucking figure... They didn't want me—they wanted the bigger fish. The bigger fish to me was my boyfriend. I know now they wanted to get to him to then get to the actual supplier, which now meant the "cartel," and I certainly wasn't "telling on them" if that's who Marcus's supplier was. I didn't actually know for sure, and I wasn't willing to take that chance regardless of who the supplier was.

I'm sure that with that large of an amount that meant the cartel. I certainly wasn't going to keep driving or help them arrest anyone else. I told them several times to please just take me to jail, and that I was not willing to do what they were asking. I don't know where the strength came from to do this, but it came with no doubt, or question whether it was right or wrong or it was best for me. The decision was made and there was no turning back.

They offered me this quote-unquote deal several times before they finally gave up. I wasn't a big enough fish to fry, and they weren't going to flip me so they turned me over to the local sheriff in a tiny city in Kansas. When they turned me over, I assumed that meant the weed also which would be the evidence if there was a case brought against me. I overheard the local officers discussing that they didn't know where to take it.

The original officer that pulled me over put me in the front seat of his cruiser, not the back this time, and drove me to the jail in that small town. The second officer drove my SUV with the weed in it, but as we were on the road he turned a different direction so I didn't know where he was taking it, and I certainly wasn't going to ask.

The officer told me that they were going to impound the vehicle and that I couldn't get anything out of it other than my purse. I could take my purse with me to jail since he retrieved it from the SUV and that was it. Not even my phone. He said that my phone, the vehicle, and the weed would all be impounded for evidence.

I cried for the first time that night, and I think I did so because the officer seemed sincerely upset and concerned for me. He didn't make me feel like he was proud to have arrested me or that he accomplished something great for himself or his town. I felt vulnerable maybe even safe with him and the tears flowed.

I was very upset not knowing what was going to happen to me. My mind was racing wondering if I made the right decision.

I quickly went from bad ass lying bitch drug mule to MOM. Because all I could think about was my teenage son back at home, and how he had no idea what I was doing, or that I was doing it mostly for him.

October 2008
Marcus How We Met

Marcus was attempting to be a football player in the NFL. As a high school football star in a small town on the East Coast, and then a big college on the East Coast, he was used to getting a lot of attention and whatever he wanted. With no support from his family, he made a lot of mistakes with his football career. Once predicted to be a first-round draft pick quickly dwindled to no draft and no college eligibility left.

He wasn't ready to give up on football, so he made his way to Arizona, and was training with some of the Arizona Cardinal players. When I met Marcus interestingly enough I was talking to a famous football player that didn't play for the Cardinals. Why I stopped talking to him to date Marcus instead was baffling not only to me but my friends and family.

I never felt comfortable around the "famous" guy, unless we were alone. I didn't like all the attention he got especially from women, and I wasn't secure enough with myself, or the way he treated me to continue that relationship.

I was comfortable with Marcus for the most part. In the beginning that was the least of my concerns, and I must say it was love at first touch with him. Even though he wasn't famous, he "looked" famous and got that same attention from a lot of women. It didn't take long for me to feel just as insecure with him.

The night we met: I was at a popular club in Scottsdale with some of my girlfriends when I was introduced to Marcus by one of my friends who played for the Arizona Cardinals.

From the moment I touched his abs on the dance floor I was hooked, and when I say hooked, I mean I was pleasantly sexually aroused. We danced like we were making love and physical connection was instant. To this day, the best place and only place I've ever felt loved by and safe with Marcus was on a dance floor. We exchanged phone numbers later that night and saw each other again a few days later.

The first night we met up after the night club, this twenty-two-years-old boy who was lying about his age by at least one year asked me to be his girlfriend. I didn't say yes, but I didn't have to. The dance floor chemistry continued in the bedroom. He made me feel things I'd never felt. He touched me with very experienced hands. I never thought about his age while we were having sex.

What was I thinking? I was thirty-five. He was way too young for me, but somehow, this relationship formed.

The relationship was rocky to say the least from the get-go. He was twenty-two and without a doubt a player. There were so many red flags including me knowing he had multiple women and probably a girlfriend, that wasn't me, in his life.

Having multiple women was easy for him. As a beautiful, young, black man, with a physique like I had never seen, it didn't take much for him to convince me to start moving marijuana yet that didn't happen right away.

We dated for a few months. I realized but kept it to myself that whoever he was living with must have been a woman. As he never let me drop him off wherever he lived, and he never invited me to his place.

Sometimes he would have a car and sometimes he didn't. All were red flags for me. Women including myself sometimes confuse and ignore reality when they are being pleased sexually and that was definitely the case for me. He had zero potential as a provider and protector, yet I'm not sure that's what I needed or wanted in my life at the time. Regardless, sex clouded my judgment.

Mid-December 2008, he told me he was going back to the East Coast for the holidays, that he was driving back with his cousin, and that he would come back to AZ in about a month. I remember being sad that he was leaving, as we were spending a lot of time together. The night before he left, we spent the time together and it was magical.

I no longer cared about his age or that he had zero potential as a real partner.

A day or so after he left, I received a collect call from him. He said that he was in jail because he got in a car accident in Arkansas, and the police found a gun in the car. I was concerned but not surprised due to his upbringing and terrible lack of potential he was already showing. I should have ended it with him right after that call from jail, but I needed more information to make that decision.

We only talked for a few minutes before the phone cut off. I didn't hear from him for days. I was calling his phone constantly, then finally one day someone answered, but it wasn't him. It was a female claiming to be his girlfriend. I was hurt but not shocked when she claimed this, but all I really wanted was for her to tell me if he was okay. I suspected there were other women, but now I had the proof that should have ended the relationship.

She told me that he was still in jail, and that I shouldn't call back unless I wanted to send the money to bail him out of jail. I did not send money and planned on never speaking to him again…

He got out of jail a few days later. He was now blowing my phone up. I didn't answer for about a week but finally gave in, since I wanted to hear his side of the story. The first time we spoke, it was heated, and he swore that she wasn't his girlfriend. He begged me to take him back. I told him there was no point in that since he was back on the East Coast, and I wouldn't see him again and certainly wasn't going to be in a long-distance relationship with a man I didn't trust.

I stayed firm with that decision, until he showed up on my doorstep not long after that. I don't know how he got back to Arizona and I didn't care. We didn't talk about it. I believed he wanted to only be with me. I started seeing him more, and he was staying at my house more often than not.

I had season tickets for the Arizona Cardinals and was a huge fan. I'd had these tickets for a few years before I met Marcus. In 2008, the Cardinals were in the Superbowl. I remember thinking it meant something that Marcus wanted to watch the game with me. He knew how much I loved football and the Cardinals, so even though he couldn't bear to watch football, since he felt he should still be playing, he would be there for me and watch the game with me.

The Cardinals lost the game to the Steelers. I was devastated. I still am. I cried with my son right after the game, then went out to my backyard alone, sat in the grass, and cried for what seemed like forever. Marcus finally came outside, picked me up and carried me inside.

That must have been when I decided to actually let him in my heart. I was still wounded from the call I got from his "girlfriend" from jail and from my ex-boyfriend Travis letting me down and breaking my heart just about a year prior, so these feelings for Marcus were unwarranted, undeserved, and happening too fast for me.

1998
Travis

In 1998, I was doing well in the financial industry and had what I thought was a great boyfriend. He had a great "real job," courted me well with flowers, great dates, plus gave me a lot of his time which included him introducing me to his family and friends, and including me in the hobbies he had before we met. These were all green flags that showed excellent potential for a partner.

I met Travis in 1998. At the time, I was still married to James but had been separated for a few years. There wasn't a need to get a divorce from James. He was my son's father, and our break up was somewhat amicable so we just agreed on some financial things; who is gonna have our son and when, no drama, no mess.

When I met Travis, I was thriving in the financial industry moving from one company to another quickly for more money and bigger titles. Travis and I fell in love so quickly within a couple months. He asked me to get a divorce from James, and I did because I wanted to be Travis's girlfriend and that wasn't gonna happen while I was still married to James, even though at that point we were separated and it was just a piece of paper.

Travis was perfect in the beginning. One of our first dates was a Cardinals game. The date went very well. He even bought us tickets for every game for the rest of that season. He figured out right away how to win my heart. I kept those season tickets through 2008, around the same time we broke up.

Sex with Travis was good but nothing over the top or mind blowing. He was a very good-looking man, and I was physically attracted to him, but my feelings for him were because of his potential to be a good, long-term life partner. Someone to grow old with.

Everyone in my life thought Travis was the greatest guy ever and he was to everyone but me. He had some significant PTSD from Desert Storm and this started to show in forms of verbal abuse toward me, and even once it turned physical with a push, a shove, and both hands holding me in the corner while he yelled at me but nothing that left bruises. That incident was isolated, and I loved him so I thought my love and support would help him out of his PTSD but that never happened.

I'm not the type of person to share my relationship woes to family or friends, since if he did something wrong in mine or their eyes they would judge him even if I choose to forgive. I never felt the need to share my relationship problems but Travis and I definitely had them.

We dated off and on for a few years before he moved in with me.

He was renting a house with a roommate, and I owned my house so it made sense for him to move in with me. But interestingly enough and regardless of who made how much money, he never paid even half the mortgage. He paid the yard guy and the cable bill. Like a lot of couples we ultimately broke up because of money, but more specifically because when I actually needed his support financially he wasn't willing to step up.

Things were getting very bad in the financial industry in late 2007. I was working for a small broker that paid me very well, but the clients I was working with were getting fewer and fewer. I was making less and less money.

Travis and I kept a five gallon bucket of change in the main bedroom closet. It was ¾ full. It was November 2007, and I didn't have enough money to pay the mortgage, so one day while Travis was at work, I decided to count the money to see if there was enough for the mortgage payment which at the time was $1800.

I sat on the floor of our bedroom and started counting. I stopped when I reached the $1800 that I needed, but there were still a lot more coins in the bucket.

I left the money that I counted out on the floor so Travis could see it when he got home from work, and then my plan was I would ask him if I could use the money for the mortgage payment.

Not only did he say, "No" but proceeded to tell me he was saving that for something else so I couldn't use it.

We had both been contributing to the bucket for three years. I foolishly thought he might be saving the money for an engagement ring. Instead of kicking him out right then and there like I should have. I borrowed the money from a girlfriend, paid the mortgage, and hoped I'd be engaged by my birthday a couple weeks later, and then he'd maybe start paying half the mortgage in December.

Only one of those things happened. He paid half the mortgage, 1 December 2007. My heart was broken but there was still Christmas, New Year, and Valentine's Day right around the corner, so my hope continued that we would get engaged. He never asked me to marry him. I broke up with him and asked him to move out, on 15 February 2008, the day after Valentine's Day. My hope was useless.

He took the bucket of coins when he moved out, and left me with only $300 of it.

I ended up losing that house, but I never would have lost that house, or been in the position I was in, in 2008, if I would have let him stay. He would have paid half the mortgage, and I would have been fine. But I couldn't get over the fact that he wouldn't help me when I needed it the most, and I'd rather be alone than with a man like that. One who wasn't going to marry me. One who let me count coins to try to pay a bill. One who was so selfish.

To this day, I don't know what he used the coins in the bucket for, but it certainly wasn't an engagement ring for me.

2004 – Bought First Home
2008 – Lost Same Home to Foreclosure

Always striving to be a good mother, keeping my son at a good school with a good sports program was part of that. I bought the home that I did in 2004, specifically so that my son could attend a certain high school; mind you, he was only in elementary school when I bought my first house so I was thinking far ahead.

I foreclosed on that same house just a few years later, in November 2008. When I lost my job in the financial industry earlier that same year.

I lost my job, my home, my car all that year. I broke up with Travis, but I wasn't going to let my son suffer. I had to keep my son in the same school district.

January – 2009
Rental House

At the end of 2008, right about the same time I met Marcus, I decided to ask one of my girlfriends and her son to move in with us so the four of us—me, my son, her, and her son could all live together to save money.

I was very stressed over money at the time, and we were both single moms so why not. Right before my home was foreclosed on, I found a rental house in the same neighborhood. Because I applied for the house before the foreclosure my credit was good enough to get approved for the house.

The four of us lived together the four years that our boys were in high school. It worked out well for us. We got to live in a really nice house and split the cost.

Neither she nor I were able to buy a house in the same neighborhood, where I had lost my home, but somehow, we were able to rent one.

February 2009
First Test Run / Road Trip with Marcus

Not long after the Superbowl, Marcus and I were spending a lot of time together, but I started seeing long, curly, blonde hair on his clothes that clearly were not mine. This made me paranoid for good reason, and we were fighting all the time.

One night we were at Z, my favorite bar. It was a Friday night so the place was packed with beautiful women and lots of football players. Marcus and I didn't arrive together. We weren't on a date, but we were a couple. He was partially living with me. Six or seven girlfriends and I were sitting at a table, and Marcus and his friends were standing somewhere nearby. My girlfriends knew Marcus at this point, and knew he was my "man."

Some girl went right up to Marcus and gave him a hug and kiss on the cheek. She clearly wasn't someone that he just met. I was visibly upset and my girlfriends weren't having it. One of them, not even my closest girlfriend, went up to Marcus and the girl who was still standing there next to him and went off on the girl, pointing at me saying that's her man etc. etc. The girl responded by saying something like, "Then her man should act like it and stop flirting with me at the gym." I heard all of this and went over myself to cuss him out.

I think at this point one of the servers at the bar said something about, "We should take it outside."

During this time in my life my go to drink was Vodka Red Bull and it made me a raging bitch. Marcus didn't deserve any sympathy, but I just wasn't a nice person while drinking that kind of liquor or being put in that situation made it all worse.

I don't remember who followed who outside but Marcus and

I ended up in the parking lot, and I was screaming at him. Finally, my friends came out and took me away from him. We drove to a club in Scottsdale that everyone from Z would soon arrive since it was more of a dance club.

By the time we got to the other club, I was already over it and missing him. I was dancing with some random guy, but I wanted him to be Marcus. That was just the beginning of how toxic the relationship became.

Marcus ended up back at my house that same night. But after our great make up sex, he went to sleep, and I took his phone. I knew he had more than one phone, so I didn't care if that would make a difference whether he'd be able to communicate with anyone. I wanted answers and knew I'd find them in his phone. I wish I never did that, and needless to say I found out where the curly blonde hair was coming from and the drama continued.

The next day when he couldn't find his phone, since I hid it well and wasn't giving it back, we fought again.

I asked him to leave, but that didn't last long. Right in the middle of that fight, he got a phone call on his other phone that his grandma had cancer, and he needed to get home.

She is the woman who raised him and they were very close. I could see his hurt and fear and I knew he would need to go home to be with her, so our fight was instantly over.

I thought it would be best to go home with Marcus to help and support him and his family during this time, and maybe I could make some money there in the meantime since I no longer had a nine to five job.

I was having a hard time finding a new job in the financial industry, so I decided to start a side business doing hair extensions. I once paid $1200 to have my hair done, so I thought I could learn to do it myself and charge people half as much doing the same hair extensions out of my home. I'd been doing hair extensions for a few months before I met Marcus.

We decided since we would need a car, we would drive from AZ to his home town on the East Coast.

We had already started talking about the weed business, so

this was a good opportunity for a test run with nothing illegal in the car.

We didn't have a lot of money so we decided to stop in Texas where I had family, we could stay with.

The weather on this road trip was awful. It was February. The first place where the weather was terrible was New Mexico. It rained the entire state, and it wasn't just rain, it was a thunder, and lightning storm. By the time we got to Texas it was a tornado, something I never experienced let alone drove through.

My nephew lived in central Texas and worked at a gym. When we arrived, he was working. We were driving in the middle of a tornado warning. I remember pulling up to the gym, parking my car in the front fire lane, and running inside. We took cover. Everyone was yelling to get away from the glass windows. I'd never experienced anything like this in my life. We had to stay there for a couple hours before the storm finally passed, and we were able to go to my nephew's apartment. We stayed there for a couple days to let the weather pass. We checked the weather reports along the route that we were going to take, and all the weather looked bad. We needed to get home before Marcus's grandma's breast cancer surgery, so we had no choice but to get back on the road.

We eventually got back on the road and were in Arkansas, and I was driving my BMW as fast as it would go, as I was looking at a tornado that was winding parallel to us. We had the radio on listening to the local news, and I was trying to get past the tornado that was going to veer to the right directly towards us. I didn't know if I should stop or keep driving, but I chose to keep driving. I wish I would have had a camera, or a phone, or taken pictures, or video, of that tornado as we were driving simultaneously with it. With my speed racer driving skills and a very fast car, we made it past the tornado before it turned towards us.

The next few hours, the weather was okay but that didn't last long. When we got close to Tennessee, we got another tornado warning in Memphis. We made it through the majority of the downtown city, but once we reached the east side of the city the tornado warnings and sirens were everywhere. We pulled over off the highway and went to a gas station.

The attendant at the gas station was yelling at everyone in the parking lot to get inside, get down on the floor, and take cover in the bathroom. I called my mom as I was sitting on the floor in the bathroom, telling her that we were in the middle of a tornado for the second time on this trip.

We sat on the floor of the gas station for at least an hour, before we thought it was safe to continue on. The rest of the way to Marcus's home was fine as far as the weather, but apparently somewhere along the road we damaged a tire because up in the mountains on I-40 we had a blowout in the middle of the night.

We pulled to the side of the road. I called roadside assistance. While we were waiting for the tow truck an officer approached us. He was white. He offered to help Marcus change the tire, but they determined it was too dangerous due to the narrow road and soft shoulder. The officer suggested that we just wait for the tow truck. He never seemed annoyed, or bothered by me being white, and my boyfriend being black, that was surprising simply based on the state we were driving through.

The trunk of my car was open to access the spare tire. The officer even looked in there. I remember thinking at the time that we could have had weed in the car, and he wouldn't have searched or cared. He didn't search the car; he was kind, which gave me false hope for things that I would experience later.

Not long after the officer left, a tow truck arrived and towed us to a service station that was open 24/7, and they replaced the tire.

We arrived at his small hometown early the next morning. I assumed that we were going to be staying with family, but Marcus was making several phone calls. It didn't seem like anyone was willing to let us stay with them, and I didn't understand why. At this point, we didn't have money for a hotel.

Finally, his mom said we could sleep at her place for a while. I met his grandma on that same day. She was days away from her breast cancer surgery. She was kind to me. I remember instantly liking her. We stayed in that town for a couple weeks. I made some money doing hair. Then, after her surgery and we knew she was going to be okay, we went back to Arizona.

The plan from there was to start moving weed from AZ to the East Coast ASAP!

March 2009
First Weed Run in Jeep

The first time, I put weed in the car and drove east I was alone in my old beat-up 1997, Jeep Cherokee. I asked my step dad if he thought the jeep would make it all the way to the East Coast. I first bought the jeep in 1999. It was only a year old, but I sold it to my mom after I bought my first BMW.

I ended up having to buy the Jeep back from Mom because I lost my BMW to repossession years later. My step dad told me that he had taken great care of the Jeep over the years, and he definitely thought it would make it so I thought why not.

My Jeep and I got on the road with 5 lbs. of marijuana hidden between some beach towels in the back cargo area. I got out of Arizona with no issues, but New Mexico proved to be a much tougher state to get through just like the previous road trips.

The weather there was horrible. I got caught in a horrific thunderstorm again, but this time I was alone. I pulled into a rest area. It was thundering and lightning so bad that I couldn't even get out of the car. I called my mom and told her that I had just peed in a Thirst Buster cup. I couldn't believe what I was doing, but I'd been camping a lot as a kid, so I knew how to squat to pee just not actually inside a vehicle.

My mom didn't know what I had in the car with me, just that I was driving out to visit Marcus and do hair.

My mother, being my closest friend, had no idea what I was doing. My son didn't know what I was doing, no one knew what I was doing. No one knew but Marcus.

After an hour, the storm dissipated, and I made it a little bit further to my first resting point. I was driving along I-40, and I honestly don't remember what city I spent the night in, or if I got a hotel, or slept in the car; however, I do remember that the very first time I did a weed run in my Jeep Cherokee with 5 lbs. of marijuana, I got pulled over in Arkansas.

Police on major highways are apparently trained to make up reasons to pull vehicles over; which will be evident throughout this story. I wasn't speeding. I had my cruise control set. This officer never even told me why he pulled me over, but when I gave him my driver's license and registration, he said that my driver's license was suspended in Arizona.

I would have never got on the road with 5 lbs. of weed if I had known my license was suspended. The suspension was a red-light ticket that I forgot to pay.

I'm not sure where I thought this would get me, but all I could think to say to the officer was—could I drive to the nearest DMV in Arkansas to pay the ticket, or could I just get a new driver's license in AR? He said no and asked me to step out of the vehicle, since he wanted to search it.

This was my first time driving with weed in the car, and I had no idea that I could have refused and told him no, but I did what he said and got out of the car.

I had been driving for several hours and at some point during the drive, I decided to take off my bra. Being a large-breasted female, I sometimes just have to do that. There wasn't any time for me to put it back on while he was approaching my car. I was wearing a pretty see-through white t-shirt, so when he asked me to get out of the car, I was quite embarrassed.

This part of Arkansas was beautiful. I was standing on the side of the road in knee-high grass with shorts on and this see-through t-shirt with no bra. I didn't feel like the officer was staring or looking at me inappropriately, but I certainly felt like the people that were driving by were slowing down to check out what was going on.

I said a little prayer to myself asking for whoever my guardian angels were to please let him not find the marijuana. He searched around in the back of the car for a couple minutes; I swear he saw the weed and just decided to let me go. He came back over to me, told me to get in the car, and handed me back my driver's license, my registration, and a warning ticket about my suspended license.

He told me that I would be safe driving through the rest of the state. He said he would make sure of that, but he couldn't guarantee me anything if I was going further. I knew he saw the marijuana after he said that. I also realized that my white skin saved me, and that the same wouldn't have happened if I was a minority. I believe if I was a minority he would have acknowledged the weed, and he would have arrested me.

As I drove away, I was shaking so bad. I got off at the next exit and parked at the gas station because I couldn't drive.

I don't know how long I sat there before I called Marcus to tell him what happened, and that all the officer did was give me a warning ticket and let me go. I was so scared to keep driving, but somehow, Marcus convinced me to keep going.

When I arrived at my destination the next day, I barely had any money. Marcus and a friend, whom he was going into this business with, met me at a hotel and gave me money to spend the night. Marcus stayed with me at the hotel but his friend, who was actually his cousin, took the marijuana into the small town where they lived.

Unfortunately, the weed wasn't worth the money they paid for it. They were very upset, and they weren't able to pay me for bringing it, at least that's what they said. So, there I was in this small town with pretty much no money.

I had done okay the last time I did hair there, so I tried again. No one in the area was doing custom clip in or infusion hair extensions for white women, so I started making a lot of money and fast.

I set up shop in an extended stay hotel and flew back to AZ about once a week to see my son.

I was making my own money, but Marcus still wanted to sell weed. So, we went back to AZ together so he could find a good "plug" in AZ with better weed and prices. That didn't take very long.

2009
Realizing White Privilege

That trip through Arkansas was the first time I experienced white privilege. I learned very quickly from the first time I got pulled over about what to do, what not to do, etc. using my whiteness to my advantage.

I started taking loads often and was doing hair when I got there. I got more creative. I started renting different cars, one way RV rentals and taking different routes.

The key part was being on the road and being white. Marcus and I knew that was the key.

April 2009
Second Weed Run in Jeep

Walmart

The second time I made the trip with weed in my Jeep, I concealed it by stuffing it inside a box spring mattress which fit inside my Jeep, but the other part of the mattress had to go on top of my Jeep. I thought I was a genius.

I don't remember exactly how many pounds it was, maybe twenty or thirty, but my jeep smelled so bad. It wasn't wrapped very well. With one part of the mattress tied to the top of the Jeep and the other part inside, I made it about halfway to my destination, then I had a tire blowout.

I don't remember which state this was in but it was a small town. I made it to a Walmart and pulled into their auto area to get a new tire.

The stress, anxiety, and sheer panic I felt during those two hours waiting for my tire to be changed was hell. I knew the service man at the Walmart could smell the marijuana, and I swear they were going to call the police on me.

I walked around the store, went to the bathroom, at the front of the store, and was completely paranoid the entire time. Just my luck there was an armed officer walking around the store, and in my mind he was there for me. I thought for sure that man was going to arrest me. Thank God all that paranoia was just in my head.

Eventually, which to me was literally forever, I heard my name over the loudspeaker in the Walmart and made my way back to the auto area where I paid for my tire and went on my way.

Even though I was in the clear leaving Walmart, I still

thought I was going to get pulled over. That for sure they called the police on me, but they would wait to pull me over on the highway. That didn't happen.

This time was a success and I arrived with a large amount of weed. But the mechanic at Walmart took some of the weed because when Marcus weighed it after I arrived, he told me the amount was five pounds less than it should have been, and one of the wrapped pieces was missing.

Summer – 2009
Business Development

This is when we all started to make money. I wasn't seeing cash in my hand; however, Marcus was paying all the bills. I lived in a beautiful house in Arizona. He paid all the bills there, and we also had a nice apartment a couple hours away from his hometown that we used to store the weed, and I did hair there also. I was making a lot of money doing hair extensions. Life was great.

I started to enjoy the drives. I would go to the library and get audiobooks. I loved to listen to the books as I drove. There's something about driving, and listening to the books, and then creating the images in your mind of what the book is saying. The books helped pass the time.

I would pick out books that were at least twelve hours, then I would plan my day around driving for twelve hours. I got it down pretty good to where I could get there in three days and two nights, staying in hotels or rest areas. Driving twelve hours straight was hard, to do so I started taking diet pills, Phentermine, to give me the energy to keep going and honestly, twelve hours felt like nothing when I was taking those pills.

The creativity continued. I started renting one-way RVs and different vehicles, so every time I was in something different. I started bringing my dog with me. I never got caught with M in the car thank God! He was definitely a guard dog on these trips. It's like he knew I was doing something wrong, and he definitely wanted to protect me. I felt safe with him and again I never got pulled over with him in the car, so that worked out well.

The RVs trips were my favorite to this day. I want to own an RV someday. I love road trips because of these journeys, and my connection to the highway at a young age.

One time, when I had an RV Marcus removed some of the screws under a table and put 70 lbs. of marijuana underneath the cushions. We thought it was the greatest hiding place ever. That same trip there was a horrible accident on the highway in TN. M, my dog, and I had to stop for three hours not moving an inch. It was great to be in an RV; I made lunch, used the RV toilet, and even turned the engine off and took M out to pee. I never got pulled over in an RV. I should have kept on doing that...

June 2010
Second Time Arrested

Part 3

Back in Kansas, I could tell the officer felt bad, as we pulled up to a beautiful white building. It was old and it reminded me of the big homes on the East Coast, but I was in Kansas.

The building had brick steps, at least thirty of them into the main entrance but the officer took me to a side entrance. The side entrance was into the jail, and the main entrance was into the town hall. It was all in one building. By this time, it was about six a.m., and the sun was coming up.

A male deputy did my fingerprints. He seemed shocked and amazed that I was there and, at first, I noticed he was quite friendly to me. He told me that I would be assigned a public defender while he was doing my fingerprints and taking inventory of the belongings in my purse including my phone.

Before at the shed the officer told me that my phone was being impounded as evidence, but he decided to give it to the deputy processing me, so that I could write down any phone numbers that I may need before it was impounded.

Being fingerprinted was terrifying, but that wasn't the first time. I had been arrested a few months before.

January 2010
Road Trip to Cardinals Playoff Game in New Orleans

January 2010, my team the Arizona Cardinals made it to the playoffs again. They were scheduled to play the Saints in New Orleans. By this time, I no longer had season tickets, but Marcus still had connections to the Cardinals, and he was able to get me tickets to the game in New Orleans. Marcus had zero interest in football or going to a game, since he had not gotten over not having played professionally himself.

I was so excited about the game and my team going to the playoffs specially, since I still was not over them losing in the Superbowl in 2008. My girlfriend and I drove from Arizona to New Orleans.

My excuse to her for us not to fly was that a girls' road trip would be a blast and would cost less than plane tickets.

I rented a Dodge Caravan for our trip to New Orleans. There was 30 lbs. of marijuana with us. I told her I would do all the driving, but that was hard to convince her of so instead, I told her she must drive the speed limit and that we could take turns driving. I can't believe that I put her in that position. I know now how wrong that was, but at the time my confidence in what I was doing had grown immensely so it truly didn't dawn on me at the time especially, since she was also white.

We drove straight through with her and I taking turns to New Orleans. We stayed in an old spooky hotel near the Saints stadium. This was my first time driving a southern route or going through New Orleans; and the last since I noticed on this route a lot more police, and highway patrol on the I-10.

I was so nervous all night, about parking the minivan on the street in downtown New Orleans that I barely slept.

I thought for sure, someone would break in and steal the weed. I know I checked the locks on every door of the minivan a million times, before we checked into the hotel. I think my girlfriend figured it out by then, but we never talked about what was in the car. We never talked about what I was doing at all.

We went to the football game the next day.

The Saints Stadium was amazing, and even though the Cardinals lost the game, I loved the experience at that stadium and was able to forget about the weed in the minivan for a few hours.

I became a Saints fan, or at least a fan of the music, and the energy in that stadium. After the game we grabbed some chicken from Popeyes, and continued on our way to Marcus's hometown. This was another successful arrival with a good amount of weed.

My girlfriend had started dating Marcus's cousin, so her being able to see him was another way I convinced her to come on the trip. Her plan was to fly back to AZ after a couple days and she did.

January 2010
First Time Arrested, Fingerprinted, and Time in Jail

The money started adding up. Marcus and his cousin needed to go back to Arizona to re-up. I had to take the minivan back to AZ, so Marcus and his cousin drove back with me to Arizona.

My hair business was all cash and so was the weed business, so we had a large amount of cash with us. I didn't know exactly how much they had, and I remember asking Marcus to tell me how much was in the car but he was vague.

Our trip back started out good. Even halfway through the second day, we were making good time. We did not argue about anything, which was rare for us.

Even though our businesses were doing well, our relationship had become very toxic for the simple fact that he was way too young for me and not capable of being committed to any woman, not even me.

I made it my mission to prove my worthiness that somehow if I did all this for him, he would stop cheating and just love me... huge mistake.

I was doing most of the driving, since Marcus was a terrible driver and I needed to be in control of something. We were in the same silver minivan, that I had rented from Enterprise Rent-A-Car, that my girlfriend and I started this trip with.

We were on I-40 somewhere in the panhandle of Texas. It was very windy. There were tumbleweeds occasionally coming across the highway.

I swerved for one of them just a little bit. A few seconds after I swerved for the tumbleweed, I saw the red and blue lights behind me. Marcus was in the front passenger seat and his cousin was in the back seat directly behind me. I pulled over.

I was nervous but knew I hadn't done anything wrong, so I was foolishly confident that we wouldn't have any issues. What could possibly go wrong with two black men in the car with me in Texas in 2010?

The officer approached. The look on his face was indifferent; he looked concerned then delighted which was very concerning to me. I don't remember saying anything to Marcus, as we were getting pulled over. The officer asked for my license and registration then asked me why I swerved. I told him because of the tumbleweed.

Simultaneously, as he was asking the question there were tumbleweeds running across the highway. I pointed and said see just like that. So, it's not like I was making it up.

I gave him my license and registration. At the same time, another officer arrived and was approaching the passenger side of our minivan. The officer on my side asked me if the guys in the car were with me. I found the question very strange, and I'm sure the look on my face was just as strange.

I said, "Yes, this is my boyfriend and his cousin." I can't tell you what went through the officer's mind when I acknowledged that the black man sitting next to me was my boyfriend, but the look on his face said it all.

I knew at that point, from the look on his face, that at the very least we were all going to jail and that I better behave, or Marcus was gonna get shot right there in front of me.

By that time, the other officer had approached Marcus on his side, and asked them for his and his cousin's IDs. I was pissed but tried not to show it, since I didn't want to escalate the situation. I still felt I had the right to ask why, since I was the driver.

So, I did ask, "Why do you need to see their IDs?" He said he didn't have to tell me why, and he took all of our IDs and went to his cruiser.

He came back just a couple minutes later, but during those few minutes I was able to ask Marcus how much money was in the car so I could be prepared if they decided to search. He said about $25,000. I know better now, but at the time I didn't think fast enough to do the math.

There's nothing illegal about having $25,000 in a vehicle that was occupied by three people in the United States. Each person can have $10,000 without being questioned, but none of us knew what to do with what came next.

The officer came back to the car and asked me to step out of the car. I did. He asked me as he was walking me to his cruiser if there was anything illegal in the car, any large amounts of cash, drugs etc. I said, "No" as he put me in the front seat of his cruiser. Then he sat down in the car with me.

He was in the driver seat, and I was in the front passenger seat. I wasn't under arrest and didn't have handcuffs on. He said, "Are you safe, are these men hurting you?" I'm sure I looked at this man like he was crazy, since again I couldn't believe he was asking me that.

I told him, "Yes, I'm good. That's my boyfriend." He seemed completely annoyed and had no issue letting me know that with his facial expressions and body language; that he absolutely was at the very least annoyed.

I still wonder today if he thinks he was doing his job by putting me in the front seat of his car, that he was somehow protecting me from my boyfriend, who just happened to be a black man.

This white Texas highway patrol needed to protect me from my black boyfriend?

This time it wasn't my white privilege saving the day, it was his white supremacy overpowering and degrading me. I couldn't believe what was happening.

He got out of the car and as he left me sitting locked in the front seat of his cruiser. He told me he was going to search my car. Marcus and his cousin were still in the minivan with the second officer standing on the outside of the passenger side watching them.

I was still locked in the front of the cruiser. All I could do was watch as the officer opened the tailgate of the minivan. It didn't take long for him to find the money in a small suitcase. He certainly didn't count it to confirm the amount or even if it was illegal. As soon as he saw the money, he and the second officer immediately drew their guns on Marcus and his cousin.

He screamed for them to get out of the car. They did with their hands up in the air, obeying every word.

The next thing I saw was one officer with his gun drawn on them while the other was hog-tying Marcus and his cousin. He mashed their faces to the black, tar, gravel highway I-40 while I sat and watched helplessly.

Finally, they put their guns away and took Marcus and his cousin to the second officer's cruiser. The first officer then moved me from the front of his cruiser to the back and handcuffed me.

Both the officers in their separate vehicles drove us a few miles off of the highway to a huge metal garage, not a police station, with nothing anywhere near it but farmland.

They took us out of the cruisers and left handcuffs on all of us. They sat us in chairs all separated from each other several yards apart so that we couldn't talk to each other.

They took us to an office individually and questioned us.

I decided somehow that I should say all of the money was mine, and that somehow, I was protecting Marcus and his cousin. I would be able to justify having all that money from my hair business.

When they searched the minivan, they found a notebook with all my clients' information from the last few months including the amount of money each paid me. The detective that was questioning me didn't believe me. It had to be drug money since two black men were in the car which was in fact the truth, since the majority of the money did belong to them.

Other than my handwritten notes, I had no way to prove that the money was mine, plus my numbers didn't add up to the amount they counted.

After a few hours of questioning, we were officially under arrest and we were all taken to jail.

This was a first for me. I had never been arrested, never been in jail, and never been fingerprinted.

The jail was very small. I could hear Marcus and his cousin talking with other men, but I was alone in my cell—just me and four cement walls with a tiny window in the door.

Thankfully for my sake we weren't in jail for very long. Marcus's grandma posted bail for us, and we were out the next day.

The rented minivan and all the cash was impounded, so our only source of transportation was the bail bondsman. She drove us back to the minivan so that we could get our personal items that were not impounded. Then she took us to the nearest town and dropped us at a Motel 6.

Together we only had a couple hundred dollars in cash to get a hotel room, a pizza, and rent another car to get home to Arizona. Surprisingly it was cheaper to rent another car than for the three of us to take a bus.

The money that was impounded was closer to $28,000. The bail bondsman conveniently referred me to an attorney.

After returning to AZ, I had no choice but to negotiate with that attorney, compromising that if the court would be willing to drop all the charges against myself and Marcus, they could keep the money as long as it covered all of my court and attorney fees. Surprisingly enough the court accepted those terms. When I think about it now, the whole town was scamming and threatening minorities whether a law was broken or not.

Swerving for a tumbleweed isn't breaking a law, and we never should have been pulled over or searched.

Marcus and I drove back to Texas two months later, and went to court to finalize the deal I previously made with the attorney. We only met with the attorney for a few minutes, but I was amazed at how this tiny courthouse had hundreds of people lined up going through the same process, including Marcus's cousin.

I remember thinking at the time that this was some kind of strange business that the bail bondsman, the court, the cops, and attorneys were running. They were and probably still are pulling people over for no reason, content getting whatever was in the car and benefiting from it at the same time.

I felt lucky that I wasn't getting in trouble. I wasn't going to jail. The only thing I got after forfeiting the $28,000 was a hundred hours of community service, and nothing on my record.

I did a few hours of community service, helping sort food at a local food bank in AZ, but I fudged the actual hours and no one at the courthouse questioned it.

Somehow, this corrupt operation made me feel lucky that my white privilege and fast thinking prevailed—that if I wasn't in the car with Marcus and his cousin, that if it was just the two of them in that minivan; there's no way it would have turned out the same.

They would have gotten jail time or worse end of story. At least that part of the story is over.

February 2010
Back in Business

Back in AZ and with no money Marcus had to find new contacts but that didn't take long. He found a supplier that was willing to give him the product up front. That relationship built and I didn't ask too many questions about it or meet too many people, but, before I knew it, we were making money again. I was taking loads about once a month that were about hundred pounds.

Marcus still wasn't physically handing me money, but he was paying the bills. When I think about it now, I should have been negotiating my cut. I was taking all the risk but that was the point. He had protection from the police in his town. I was thinking like a girl in a toxic love relationship, like I was going to be with this man forever. I did things for the good of the relationship. He did things that benefited him. I know now at the very least I was being taken advantage of.

June 2010
Second Time Arrested

Part 4

After the sheriff deputy in Kansas finished fingerprinting me, he told me that I would be assigned a public defender if I didn't have an Attorney, I did not. He walked me to my cell, and even though I had been in a jail cell before nothing could have prepared me for these next five days.

The building was old and very large. Combining all of the city's government entities in one building. As I walked to what would be my cell for the next five days, he told me that there hadn't been a woman in that jail before that looked like me...

I could see men in cells as I was walking past. They were heckling at me, so I looked down and didn't make eye contact with them. I remember the deputy telling me that two of the men I went by were from Canada, and they'd gotten caught with almost a thousand pounds of marijuana. I don't know why he told me that or whatever happened to those men. I could hear them talking for a day or so, but then the jail got quiet and it was just me.

Early Friday morning, the deputy warned me that it would be at least Monday before a judge would determine my bail, and he couldn't tell me when I'd be able to see a public defender.

There was a pay phone in my cell that I could make collect calls on, a shower, a toilet, a bunk bed, and TV. There was a large window with bars that looked down at the front of the building. I was right in the middle directly above those thirty steps. I could see the street, and houses, and people coming, and going all from that window. The room was large, maybe 300 square feet. I took it all in and tried not to completely lose it.

I was exhausted from being awake all night, but I couldn't sleep. I called my mom, and told her I was in jail. I think deep down she knew what I was doing but we just didn't talk about it.

She was devastated, but this wasn't the first time one of her children called from jail. Both of my brothers had been arrested, but as a Mother you don't think about your daughter being arrested or being in jail.

Having to call my mom and put that kind of stress on her was gut wrenching. I think I called Marcus's cell phone, but wasn't able to talk to him. I finally got through to his grandma to let her know I was in jail.

All I could think about was my son, and what was going to happen to me, how could I pull this off without letting him find out. He was in high school at the time, and he had no clue what I was doing.

Nothing happened that Friday. It was the longest weekend of my life. I tried watching TV. The TV only got two channels, a weather channel and another channel that was playing *The Big Bang Theory* over and over. I was interested in the weather channel because there was a tornado moving through our area in Kansas. I remember thinking this old building was sturdy and that I would be fine. We don't have tornadoes in Arizona, so just thinking about experiencing yet being indoors and not in a moving car was intriguing to me. My only other tornado experience was the one I raced in my car the prior year, my nephew's gym and the gas station in Memphis.

Anything to take my mind off of what was going to happen to me. At some point I must have slept. I moved back and forth from the top and the bottom bunk to see which one was more comfortable, but they were both awful. The mattress wasn't more than two inches thick, so basically sleeping on springs. I even tried the floor on Saturday, but the floor and the walls were all concrete. The floor was concrete gray, and the walls were bright white, the complete opposite of relaxing.

The same deputy that had taken my fingerprints came into my cell. He brought me a bucket, a white t-shirt, and some bleach. He told me to scrub the walls.

I had to remove my bra the first day, since it had an underwire. The jump suit they provided me was separated, a blue top and bottom. The material was thick so the no bra wasn't a huge problem plus they didn't have anything small enough for me, so I had to roll the waistband of the pants. The shirt wasn't too big, but just enough room to not be tight around my breast.

I knew there were cameras in my cell. I knew the deputy could watch me, but I did what he said, put the white tee on and scrubbed the walls. I was very careful when I changed the shirt, to keep my back to the camera and made sure not to get my t-shirt wet. While I was scrubbing, I kept my back to the camera as much as I could. I was not going to let this man get satisfaction watching me. I could tell that he didn't like that. I out-smarted him, when he came back to retrieve the bucket and tee shirt with it written all over his face.

The worst part was the bleach. I didn't realize it until years later, but I'm allergic to bleach and it is a trigger for me to have a severe migraine. I'd had a migraine before but not like this. I was in so much pain clearly from the bleach and stress of the whole situation, but all the deputy would give me was aspirin, which did nothing. I begged him for something stronger and actually migraine specific but he refused.

Later, he brought me a razor, a small towel, and soap. Like it was a consolation prize, for not properly treating my migraine. He said I wasn't allowed to have razors, but if I wanted to shave I could. I'm not a hairy person. I could go weeks and you still couldn't see the hairs on my legs, so I could care less about shaving.

The shower was in the corner of the cell on the same wall with the cell door. The camera could capture the entire room. I think he thought that when I accepted the razor that I would completely undress outside of the shower. He could get a good look at me this time, but I outsmarted him again. I went into the shower fully dressed, removed my clothes in the shower, and set the clothes outside the shower. I took a long hot shower.

The shower did make me feel slightly better, but I still had a migraine. I dried off in the shower with the tiny white towel the deputy provided me, when he gave me the razor and the bar of soap.

I put my blue jail suit back on in the shower; all behind the curtain so he never got a chance to see me naked. I refused to give him the satisfaction. Maybe he got off on seeing me pee, since there was no way for me to hide that. The toilet was in the open, right next to the pay phone, and directly in front of the camera.

I think he knew that I figured out his plan to see me naked. He mentioned that there had never been a woman in their jail before. I felt violated, but what could I do about it? I had no power in this situation and he knew that.

Sunday came and the actual sheriff of the town came to see me. The sheriff didn't walk into my cell like the deputy did when he brought me food, or bleach, or a razor, he just opened the window of the cell door.

He told me that he spoke to my mother and that she was going to "put up" her 1955 Buick to bail me out.

I don't know why he told me that. First of all, the fact that my mom would do that for me was great but certainly wasn't her responsibility. This seemed strange to me, since this sheriff was looking at me like he's just won the lottery.

The DEA turned me over to him including the 364 lbs. of marijuana. That's winning the lottery for a small-town sheriff, since it was evidence, he could do what he wanted with it.

My mom never used her car to bail me out. Marcus and his cartel buddies were somehow grateful, or scared, to leave me in jail too long, that I would rat them out. My bond was 30K so coming up with $3,000 wasn't a lot.

The night before, the deputy who had been there all weekend and the one who had been bringing me three meals a day. Along with his tactics to get me naked decided to be nice by bringing me fried chicken.

He said his mom made it. It was better than anything else that he had given me as far as food. It was very good and after nibbling on peanut butter and jelly sandwiches for the last two days a hot meal was welcomed.

Maybe he felt guilty and figured I knew he was trying to watch me in an inappropriate way. How he thought the fried chicken was going to make up for that is beyond me, but I ate it gratefully. Monday morning, a female public defender came and got me out of my cell.

I met with her in a small office, the same room, where I was fingerprinted.

She told me what my bond was, and that the bail bondsman would most likely receive the money that was required that day, and that I would be out the next day on bail until trial.

I told her about the deputy and him watching me. I told her about the sheriff and how he looked at me. I told her about the DEA and the six hours they interrogated me. I told her about the initial officer that pulled me over and how my vehicle was searched when I was at the gas station. To this day, I don't know if any of those things were a factor regarding my charges or if it was just my white privilege.

Tuesday morning, five days after being jailed a bail bondsman came and got me out. He was a very nice man. I didn't feel like he was part of any scam like what I felt in Texas at least from him. He even told me that I had the right to refuse to have my vehicle searched. That the officer that took my keys to the vehicle in exchange for allowing me to use the restroom at the gas stations was unlawful. That the search was illegal, and that could help me in court. He drove me to Walmart to buy a burner phone, since my phone was impounded for evidence and not returned to me. He took me to the black Suburban that I was driving. There were a few personal items still in there that were not impounded, that I was able to get back. After that, he dropped me off at the nearest bus station.

I had asked for my cell phone back, but the deputy that released me to the bail bondsman said it was evidence and that it would be returned to me after court.

I got to the bus station several hours before the bus was leaving. I was sitting at a picnic bench, outside the bus station which was actually a gas station, still not knowing what was going to happen to me but grateful to be out of jail.

June 2010
The Breakup with Marcus

I was looking forward to the long bus ride back to Arizona, and I hoped I would get a window seat, so I could see out. Ever since I was a child, on road trips with my family, I had to be near a window to look out or I would get car sick. Then as an adult, I always preferred to be the driver to avoid getting car sick. Once, I got settled in my window seat. I tried calling Marcus from my burner phone, but he didn't answer like most people who don't answer their phones if they don't recognize the number. I called his grandma's phone. She picked up. I talked to her for just a few minutes and asked her to give him the number. I knew he was sitting right next to her but didn't want to talk to me. Marcus apparently decided not to trust me. He knew that I would be getting out of jail since he arranged the bail. But he must have thought I was working with the police, and that's why my bail was so low, and I was out.

I couldn't believe that after what I did to protect him, he wouldn't even speak to me. At some point during the bus ride back to Arizona he spoke to me for a few minutes but he was vague, and cruel, and distant. I was alone and devastated.

I thought how ungrateful he was, and that made me question why I didn't just keep on driving like the DEA asked me to and let them arrest him instead of me.

A couple weeks went by with zero communication from Marcus.

I decided I needed to go to him and talk to him face-to-face. I got on a plane, then rented a car when I arrived. I had to fly into a bigger city then drive to the small town he was from. I drove right to that small town after my red eye flight that I didn't sleep a wink on.

I was exhausted, but I had to see him. I think he must have thought that I was still going to turn him in, that I was wearing a wire, or had police outside with me because he still pushed me away. He even went so far as to break up with me. He told me he didn't want to be with me anymore. I remember we were sitting in my rental car parked at the lake near his grandma's house, since he wouldn't let me in their house. That's how and where he broke up with me. In a car, but at least it was face-to-face and not over the phone. I got what I came for... closure. I wish our relationship had truly ended that day, but it did not.

No man had ever initiated a break-up with me. It was always me making that decision, and I didn't know how to deal with it.

I was devastated, crying, and in tears, begging him not to break-up with me and to believe me. That I wasn't working with the DEA, or any police, if I would have been they would have already arrested him. None of that mattered to him.

My ego was damaged, and any insecurity I had regarding Marcus tripled that day. I'd gone to jail for this man twice and he had zero appreciation.

After our short conversation / breakup, I drove back to our apartment closer to the airport. He wasn't staying there, since that was our meeting point and storage for the weed. I spent a few days alone crying and doing hair to make enough money to last me a little while, since now I'd have to pay all my own bills. I couldn't count on him anymore. I'd have to go back to Arizona to be with my son before school started back up, so I needed to make as much money as possible before I returned.

During that time in the apartment alone, I did some research to see what a black man or rather any person would be sentenced to for doing something similar to what I got caught with. What I found was a fifteen year minimum approximate sentence. The information I found was confusing and different in every state, so I looked specifically at Kansas and all I could find was that I'd definitely be getting jail time if the Judge allowed the evidence. This is what I thought I was facing. All I could think about was what a mistake I had made, and that I should have let the DEA arrest Marcus and I would be free. Now my fate was in the hands of a small-town sheriff, a judge, and a public defender, since I had no money for a good defense attorney. Marcus and his cartel supplier were no longer helping me.

I was given a court date for about six weeks later, sometime in July. I was able to communicate with my public defender via email, and she initially told me that the prosecutor offered a plea deal of a Felony 10, and I had no clue what that meant. I did more research online, and found that a Felony in Kansas would include jail time from five months to three years, which sent me into a panic. I questioned her and reminded her about what I believed was an illegal search, and my treatment while I was in jail by the deputy, that I didn't have a prior record etc. and that I thought the case should be dismissed or be a misdemeanor at most. She went on to say that she was trying to get the evidence thrown out (the weed) due to the illegal search. I never heard back from her regarding what the plea was going to be until I arrived in Kansas the night before my hearing. I spent weeks agonizing over my fate, and only had my mom to talk about it.

July 2010
Court in Kansas

I'm not sure how I even paid for the plane ticket back to Kansas, since it was impossible to work while being that stressed out. I had to fly through Dallas for a connection. The plane, the airport, and the town that I was going back to were all very small, and I still was thirty minutes away from where I was in jail and where I was going back to court; the same building that I was jailed in.

When I landed at the tiny airport, I didn't know what to expect. I arrived a day early to be extra responsible and not miss court. My plan was to just get there, rent a car, and get a cheap hotel. Then drive to the courthouse thirty miles away the next day.

Since I previously had two rental cars impounded when I was arrested, one from Enterprise and one from Dollar, I couldn't rent a car from them or any of their affiliates.

Again, this being a tiny airport, there were only a couple places to rent cars Enterprise and Avis. I didn't bother with Enterprise, so I made a reservation with Avis before I left home. When I arrived at the counter, I was surprised at the amount they wanted to charge in addition to the daily fee. I was trying to use my debit card but it declined. They gave me an option to run my credit and I agreed but figured that still wouldn't get me approved for a car, since I wasn't paying bills on time including my mortgage. I knew my credit was terrible.

I was denied a car, and didn't know how I was going to get to a hotel or to court the next day. No Uber in 2010, certainly not in that tiny town. I went out to the curb of the airport, and the fact that I was in a tiny middle of nowhere tiny town/airport was evident.

There were no taxis to be found, so I sat on a bench and cried outside the airport. I called my mom for comfort, but there was nothing she could do for me. I looked at a bus stop but didn't see any buses and even considered just walking, but even then the technology on our phones is nothing like it is today. No walking GPS.

I'm not sure how much time had passed or if I was still crying when my hero arrived. A small red car approached me. The man rolled down his window, and asked me if I needed a ride. I said, "No, thank you." I certainly wasn't getting in a car with a strange man, but he continued and said that he just dropped off his friend, and he could take me to town if that was where I was headed. Again, I said no thank you and that I would wait for a taxi. He then pulled out his military ID and said there wouldn't be a taxi coming anytime soon, if at all, and that I could hold his ID during the ride.

I'm not sure why I decided to trust this young man, but I decided to take him up on his offer. Before the thirty-minute drive, I texted a picture of his military ID to my mom to make her and I both feel better about accepting his help. I explained why I was there, and he listened politely. He even said he'd take me to court the next day if I needed him to. He gave me his phone number to call him if I needed that.

I was still leery of him so I had him drop me off in a shopping center, near a couple hotels, so he wouldn't know exactly where I was staying. I only had a small overnight bag with me, so it was no issue walking a few blocks to a hotel.

Thankfully, I didn't have any issues getting a hotel like I did with a car. I checked into the room, and called my mom to let her know I was safe.

The next phone call was to my bail bondsman, since he was responsible for me. I thought he might be able to get me to court. We arranged for him to pick me up at my hotel, wait for me while I was in court, then he would take me to the airport for my flight back to Arizona, which was all the next day. I don't remember if he charged me extra for that but he must have.

Then I called my public defender. I hadn't had any communication with her since the email a couple weeks prior.

She was kind and she said that she got me a deal where I would get time served, my five days in jail and pay a $500 fine, and that I would be on probation for six months. She never told me if she got the evidence thrown out, but she must have because the plea was no longer a felony. She only told me that this offer was great, not a felony, and that I should take it. I told her I would accept the offer. But it was still insane to me. I thought I was facing actual jail time. Then *poof*... NOTHING! Can you imagine my relief? She told me that walking into the courtroom and pleading guilty was just a formality!

I wondered how this public defender, not a fancy high-paid lawyer, got me this deal and how did anyone get paid when my fine was only $500?

That three hundred and sixty-four pounds of weed, the evidence, apparently took care of them all. I don't think I slept in that hotel room. I kept going over and over in my mind that the deal I was getting could not be possible. I figured once I go to court the next day something would change, and I would be getting jail time.

I spent the night thinking about having to tell my son I was going to prison. He didn't even know where I was that night, that I was going to court, or that I'd ever been arrested for anything.

I walked into a small courtroom with just me, my public defender, the prosecutor, and the Judge. I plead guilty, and the Judge accepted the terms that were pre-arranged prior to that day. I don't remember the faces of everyone I came across during this journey, but I remember his. My last name was the same as the Judge. It seemed like they all felt sorry for me, but the feeling was similar to when I was in court in Texas. Somehow, they were all benefiting from my mistakes so that the "evidence" would benefit all of them, and that was why my plea deal was so good.

The prosecutor was the only one who seemed to not be on my side or not benefiting from me. But maybe it was just a planned act, so I wouldn't be suspicious regarding their scam or at least in my mind it seemed like a scam.

He tried to bring up my previous occurrence in Texas. I don't know how he even knew about that, since it wasn't on my record.

The Judge dismissed him right away, and said that our deal was already made up-front and he was going to agree with it. When the Judge actually confirmed my sentence, matching what the public defender told me, I was relieved to say the least and once again grateful that I wasn't going to jail.

I walked out of the courthouse, down those same thirty steps that I stared at for five days while I was in jail, while my heart leaped with joy.

The actual relief that I felt was overwhelming. I still didn't know exactly why the deal was so good, but I do know that from the moment the officer pulled me over, being white was a huge factor.

I got back in the car with the bail bondsman less than an hour later, and he took me back to the airport. I had to sit there a few hours before my flight which felt like days. I couldn't wait to get back to Arizona and give my son the biggest hug ever.

I waited to contact Marcus until I got home, since I didn't think he even cared what happened to me. I eventually told him the deal that I got. You would think we would have celebrated together, that he would honor and acknowledge that I was protecting him, but that didn't happen right away.

He was still cruel and vague with me. I don't think he believed that I was able to get that good of a deal without giving him up, and that I did turn him in and he'd be arrested soon after. He started this whole plan to move weed, knowing that me being white would benefit him if anything ever went wrong. Him refusing to acknowledge this was beyond me, since it was the same reason I got such a good plea. He didn't trust his own judgment from the past and didn't trust me.

He continued that behavior and kept his distance from me for a few months, but we eventually started speaking again and we made up.

Fall 2010
Done Being a Drug Mule

I knew that I would never be involved in his business again, and I hoped he would be done with it as well. Being arrested two times and spending a total of six nights in jail was enough for me to realize that it wasn't worth it. I loved my son more than any man, and would never risk going to jail or being away from him again. Period!

I couldn't make as much money in Arizona doing hair extensions as I did on the East Coast. There were too many salons doing it in AZ, and I didn't have enough clients to pay the bills.

Marcus certainly wasn't paying any of my bills and the apartment back east was gone, so I couldn't go there to make money, or justify the expense for a hotel room, or flight.

I started looking for other jobs while I continued to do hair extensions, when I could to make money. Marcus must have realized I didn't turn him in, and we started talking often on the phone. During one of our conversations, he suggested that I apply for a job at an airline. A friend told him about flight benefits, and over the last couple years we had spent a lot of money on flights, so having a girlfriend that worked for an airline would be very convenient for him, as we were most likely going to start seeing each other again. Free flights would benefit us, since we lived in two different cities across the country.

We never really discussed that we were getting back together, but we eventually did.

December 2010
Applying to Be a Flight Attendant

I am absolutely in love with my job and my career as a flight attendant, however I'm not one of those people who dreamed of being a flight attendant. Sometimes, I feel guilty because there are so many people that would love to have this job and I just stumbled onto it.

After that conversation with Marcus, I applied for three different positions at a major airline that had a base in PHX.

I had some friends that were already flight attendants, but I didn't tell them that I was going to apply for an airline job. I wanted to try to do it and see what happened.

The first job I applied for was a reservation agent part time. I thought that I could do that, and hair extensions have flight benefits, and that would be perfect. I also applied for a corporate sales job, and with my experience in the financial industry I thought for sure I qualified for that position. But just in case, I also applied for a flight attendant position.

I got three response emails from the airline—one saying that I was overqualified for the customer service rep, one that I was under qualified for the sales job, and the third said they wanted me to continue to apply for the flight attendant position.

I can't even remember if I was excited. I think I was just happy to be considered for any airline job. The pay rate was at $16/hr. I made a lot more than that doing hair extensions. Plus being a mule for Marcus paid all my bills. Thinking about making $16/hr. was concerning.

I didn't know anything about the airline industry. I didn't even know that $16/hr. really meant $8, since flight attendants only got paid while on the plane.

Prior to the hair and running weed days I was in the financial industry where in my last job, in 2007, I made six figures. Applying for a job where I was going to make pennies didn't sit well with me, but I decided to try just to prove to myself that I could get hired, and that maybe after that I wouldn't be able to afford to take the job.

Beginning 2011
Flight Attendant Interview

The first interview after the email was a phone interview. I passed that interview in the beginning of January 2011, and then I was told that I had to go to a face-to-face interview in Phoenix at the airlines training facility.

I was given instructions for the interview—including that it would take several hours, to pack a lunch, bring a book, and what to wear. But even with those instructions, I certainly wasn't prepared for what I walked into.

There were at least a hundred people there to be interviewed. It was set up like *American Idol*. People were getting cut every round.

I made it past the first round, where they made us reach up into an overhead bin of a mock airplane, and pull out a suitcase. Easy!

I made it past the round where they made us sit in a jump seat (I didn't know what a jump seat was) and put the seat belt around my shoulders and waist.

I made it through the individual interview, where they asked me what my best customer service experience was. I said something about helping someone get their credit score up—so they could buy a house, and that I had to work with these people for four months, and that I helped them get their dream home. It was true and I actually did that several times in the thirteen years I was in the financial industry.

All of those rounds were easy for me.

The only thing that was hard for me was when there were a hundred of us in the room, and they made us stand up individually. We had to say four or five different things within one minute—name, where we were from, why we wanted to be a flight attendant etc. Standing up in front of all those people was very scary to me, but somehow, I did it. Then somehow, I made it to the final round. They split us into groups. There were only about twenty people left, as people were being cut every round. They instructed us to work together as a team, that we were in a scenario as if we crashed on a desert island. We had a set of items/tools and could use them, so we could work together to decide which of these items we would use, and how we would use them so we could survive or be rescued.

I know now it really wasn't about the items or how to use them, it was just about teamwork and who is going to be a leader.

I took charge right away asking the group questions and opinions about the items. This exercise went on for about ten minutes while the instructors watched us. Needless to say, I made it past the final test of the day.

The same day, about an hour later, only six of us were left in the room.

We were all just sitting there talking, wondering what was next. Finally, an instructor came into the room and said that we were all hired, and we were going to be fingerprinted for an FBI background check right then and there.

It was mid-February 2011. My heart stopped since it was only about eight months after I had been arrested, been in jail and court, so I still wasn't sure whether something would show up on my record or not. I didn't know how to check myself but it was too late for that.

I really didn't know what would show up if anything. I figured that an FBI background check must be different, certainly more detailed than a regular one, and that I would never be able to get this job.

I was so nervous, but I wasn't going to NOT let them fingerprint me.

My emotions were all over the place, wanting to be thrilled that I was hired, but couldn't get my hopes up.

I called Marcus as soon as I left, and told him that there's no way I was going to get hired. This was the first time he truly acknowledged what I did for him. I heard gratitude in his voice for the first time. He said that if I somehow didn't get the job because of things that I had done to help him, he would never forgive himself.

Maybe that's when I fell back in love with him, or at least opened my heart to him again. I felt good when he said that, but it really wouldn't have been his fault. I still did everything I did knowing that if I got caught there could be consequences. I just didn't know specifically what they would be.

Once my fingerprints were done, the instructor said the next step was a drug test and that I had to go to an airline doctor, and that was scheduled for the next day.

That was the last thing I was worried about. I don't do any drugs, with all the time being around marijuana, it's not something that's ever been interesting to me. Weed was simply a source of income.

February 2011
Waiting for FBI Background Check

The next two weeks, waiting for the results from the FBI background check were torture. I went from being concerned about how much money I would or wouldn't be making, to absolutely wanting to be a flight attendant.

Maybe again to prove something to myself, yet not knowing for many years later that I was actually proving that white people in this country are privileged simply for the color of their skin.

What seemed like years was actually about two weeks. It's now the beginning of March 2011.

My background check came back clean, and they wanted me to start training right away.

I could choose to start training in April or May 2011. I decided to put my training off until the end of May, so I could be home for this last month of my son's school year.

I knew training would be intense. I didn't know anything about the airline industry. I had no idea what to expect.

May 2011
Flight Attendant Training

My flight attendant training was scheduled for five weeks and was in Arizona, but since there was always a lot of noise and hectic stuff going on with two teenage boys and a roommate in the house. I decided it would be best for me to stay at the hotel that the airline was providing.

I had to study every night after class. I had no idea what I was getting myself into. There were about sixty of us going through training together. Training wasn't easy for me. We were in class eight hours a day preparing for the weekly test.

We had to pass the test at ninety percent or better. I was an okay student as a child, but I never really tried hard or had anyone push me to learn or study.

Studying wasn't something I ever remember doing as a child and certainly not in high school. I decided that I must study every night after class. I wanted this now, still proving to myself that I could do this.

I was one of the older trainees at thirty-eight, although there were a few people older than me, most were younger. The younger trainees wanted to party and hang out, and all I wanted to do was study. All the studying paid off because I passed all of my tests and graduated with flying colors!

June 2011 – And Beyond
First Few Years as a Flight Attendant

Becoming a flight attendant and going through training was difficult for me but actually being a flight attendant was not. I quickly became a very good flight attendant, only wanting to work first class and being the lead flight attendant.

The first few years were very difficult; making $16/hr. proved to be harder than I could have even imagined. I was also on reserve, meaning I never knew my schedule. I had a two-hour call out to get to the airport for a flight. Sometimes, I worked one flight a day; sometimes, I worked four.

I was always tired and stressed out as a new flight attendant. I never got weekends or holidays off, so I spent many holidays away from my friends and family. My first Thanksgiving I spent alone in a hotel room in Salt Lake City, calling my mom and crying.

Those first couple years, I was able to have a part-time job working with my mom at the company she worked for, doing accounting and bookkeeping. This was something that came easy to me. Numbers were always my thing, especially after being in the financial industry.

Marcus and I continued to see each other, but he lived on the East Coast and I lived in Arizona. I put him on my flight benefits so that we could travel back and forth to see each other. I bid on a lot of trips that took me to the East Coast so that we could see each other.

Summer – 2015
Transferred Bases to be with Marcus

Our relationship continued to be toxic, and I decided that the only way we were going to be able to continue this relationship was if we were in the same city.

He had turned his drug money into a legitimate business, as a personal trainer and model. As a flight attendant we are able to transfer to bases, so I decided to transfer to the closest airport to him and move out there.

It was the end of 2015. I packed everything that I could fit in my C300 Mercedes, including my dog M and moved to the East Coast to be with Marcus.

When I first got there, I stayed with Marcus and his family since he didn't have a place of his own, at least that's what he told me.

After being there for about a week, we found an apartment together.

I was still on reserve out there, but I wasn't flying very much. I was only collecting the guaranteed money that the airline gave me, and Marcus was again paying the majority of the bills. The small apartment didn't work well for my dog M, so we started looking for houses.

I started noticing that every time I went to work on a trip, things were different in the apartment when I came back. The pictures of my son were put into a drawer, and my clothes were all in a closet with the door closed.

I started questioning him, and he basically said that his grandma had come and cleaned the apartment, and that's why the things were put away. That made no sense and I knew something was off.

I knew better. I knew that a female had been in our

apartment. I knew that he had brought a female around my dog, and somehow that felt even worse.

It didn't take me very long to realize that he actually had another girlfriend out there and was living a double life. Everything became very toxic, to the point where it turned physically abusive. The neighbors called the police on him during one of our fights. They could hear us fighting about this other woman. I was confronting him, and the argument got so heated that he pushed me across the room and grabbed me around the throat. He never punched me or slapped me, but I was afraid of him; screaming and crying loud enough that the neighbors called the police.

I didn't know that the neighbors had called the police, but somehow, he did because he left before the police arrived.

I called his female cousin right about the same time the neighbors must have called the police because she arrived the same time as the police. She was there with me when the police asked me if I wanted to press charges. I told them yes, and then she went with me to the stations to file charges against him. She and I had become friends over the last couple years, but the friendship developed more once I was living in the same city. She knew Marcus was cheating, and I think she felt sorry for me plus she made it clear that she liked me better for Marcus than the other woman. But, even with her seeming to be on my side when it came to Marcus, she was still his blood and I was the outsider so this friendship gave me no advantage.

While we were at the police station she was on the phone with Marcus, and he was telling her to ask me not to file the charges since that would activate a warrant for his arrest. I filed the charges regardless, and the warrant was issued.

He came to the apartment every day begging me to let him in, so that he could say sorry. I gave in a few days before the court date arrived. I dropped the charges; we made up and I forgave him or at least I thought I did.

The apartment complex wasn't okay with what happened and suggested that we move out.

I found a large beautiful home for us to rent, with a fenced backyard that was going to be perfect for my dog. Marcus knew I wasn't happy, and that I didn't trust him, but he was willing to do anything to make it work.

I told him that I wanted this new house to be my home, our home and I needed all my things, all my furniture and household things from my storage in Arizona.

I only had the things that fit in my car, when I first drove out. I wanted all of my things so that our home looked like a female lived there, so that he wouldn't be able to bring a female to my home when I was working.

His cousin, who was my friend, flew back to Arizona with me. This was the first time she had ever been on an airplane. She was scared to death.

She cried as the plane was taking off, but I was grateful that she came with me.

We spent a couple days in Arizona visiting my family, and then we packed everything in a Penske truck, and we drove from Arizona to the East Coast. I had made this trip many times before but had never driven in a vehicle that big. One of the RVs might have been close. During the drive I was thinking how easy it was to drive that truck, and had the thoughts again of being a truck driver in a past life, my current life, and maybe even in the future. I liked being a flight attendant, but I liked being on the road more than the sky. I knew that then as I know it now.

I did all of the driving. She was just there for moral support.

We arrived back at my new home a few days later, and as I got settled, I felt a lot better being in the larger home, and having all of my things there.

Nothing changed, every time I went to work. I worried about Marcus bringing a woman into our home. I knew that every time I left there was a woman around. The house would be clean and he never cleaned.

His grandma would always come clean up and get rid of any evidence that another woman had been there.

I remember not wanting to go to work because I figured every time that I did, he would be cheating on me.

I went on a trip for work in late October 2016. I was in the air, done with my FA duties, and on a short break. I opened my FB and saw a post from his cousin, my friend. The post read that it was the worst day of her life. I messaged her right away to ask what was going on, and she told me that her brother had died. He was twenty-two.

I never felt completely comfortable with anyone in his family, even though I tried with his cousin. Sometimes they looked at me like I was an alien, and why was I there.

I kept my distance when needed and as much as possible. Since I didn't trust Marcus, I did not trust any of them. My dog and his family were all I had in that small town, so I tried to make the best of it. My family and friends were twenty-three thousand miles away.

We lived in the town he was from, where he was born and raised. Everyone in the town knew who he was, even the police. Every girl wanted him, even one of his female first cousins.

Everyone hated me, or at least it seemed that way. The white woman from the other side of the country, somewhere none of them had been. My name was constantly the topic of gossip.

I realized years later that the hate wasn't about me, it was just a hateful place, period—family hated family. Friends hated on friends. Enemies hated on enemies. The negativity, drama, and gossip in the town was exhausting. It was impossible to establish a healthy relationship with Marcus in that city.

The majority of his family lived in this small country town, some of them never even leaving the state. This town was racially divided by actual railroad tracks. There weren't any white people on his family's side of the tracks, so I stuck out like a sore thumb. The house I chose for us to live in was several miles away, on the "white people" side of the tracks.

I don't remember anyone ever particularly being rude to my face, but I knew that they were talking about me behind my back. I knew they hated that Marcus, the most successful man in their family, was with a white woman. They wanted us to fail, and they actively participated in making that happen.

I knew that his grandma was essentially helping him cheat on me. What kind of woman does that?

I tolerated this treatment for about a year.

The nail in the coffin was the day of his twenty-two-years-old cousin's funeral.

The night before the funeral, we were all at a family member's house. Gathering together, neighbors, and friends brought flowers and food for the family.

I felt like a complete stranger there, no one embraced me. There were hundreds of people coming and going. I didn't even know where Marcus was most of the night, but he wasn't by my side.

I remember feeling so completely out of place. At some point I found him. I was sitting in the living room, looking out the window, when I saw him hugging a woman. This wasn't a friendly or family hug. It lasted too long and looked too sexual, but I thought maybe it was just me seeing through my not trusting eyes.

Turns out the female was family. She was the first cousin who didn't care who knew, or how strange it was that she wanted him.

As I sat there and watched, someone made a comment about her to me. Then the two of them walked in the house together. She looked right at me and said, "So, you're the white girlfriend?"

Marcus said nothing, and neither did I. I just rolled my eyes, sat there and said nothing, not my personality at all. I wanted to get up and beat her ass or his, but clearly that wasn't going to happen. No one in the family would have had my back including Marcus, and I would have been the one getting beat up.

Instead, I got up and asked him for the keys to our car. We had tequila in the car, and I said I needed to get a drink. He gave me the keys, and I walked down the street where the car was parked. I got in and left. I went home alone. I left him there. A couple hours later he realized I was gone and he started calling and texting me. I never answered. I knew he could find a way home, or not come home at all, either way I didn't care. That night I made my plans to return to AZ, as soon as my lease on our home was up, which wasn't for a few months but I needed a plan to leave.

The next day at the funeral, Marcus and I drove to the funeral home together, but when we got there, and as the family gathered to go into the funeral home, apparently there was a plan as to who was walking in with who and that didn't include me.

He walked away from me, grabbed his grandmother's hand and walked her in, leaving me standing there alone.

I understood that was a horrible day for his grandma being the matriarch of the family. It made sense for him being her closest grandson, that he would walk with her as she wasn't married and needed the support, but no one told me that was going to happen, that I wouldn't be included or considered as his partner.

This all happened very fast and before I realized what was happening, hundreds of people were walking into the funeral home and I was no longer with the family.

I sat alone at least fifteen rows behind the family. He never even turned around to see where I was.

The service was very long, sad, and emotional. I was sobbing. An usher brought me tissue, but the loss I was grieving was more about me and Marcus.

It ended for me emotionally right then and there. I would never give my heart to him again. I saw him for exactly who he was and wasn't. He didn't love me, that was clear, and I knew he never would. I don't know why it took that day for me to finally realize it after everything he had already put me through, but I knew that it was over for us.

When the service was over, I went back to our car which was parked directly behind the one limo that was for family and the horse and carriage that would carry the coffin to the graveyard a few miles away.

I didn't know about the car arrangement, or that it was also planned like that the night before. I was just standing outside the car since he had the keys.

When he got to the car, he could tell I was upset, but instead of apologizing he yelled at me and said that everyone at the service just saw us get in the car together, and that everyone knew we were together; that it shouldn't be that big of a deal that we didn't sit together for the service.

The night before when I was home alone, I put in my transfer back to AZ, and I booked a Penske truck back to Arizona for March when my lease on the house would expire.

The next few months were awful. I knew that the relationship was over. I knew that I was leaving, but I never told him. We tolerated each other, but I think we both knew that it was over.

March 2017
The Move Back Home

When I was ready to move back in March, my mom flew out from Arizona so that she could drive back with me to Arizona. Even though I had driven, and done road trips alone many times I didn't want to be alone. I knew the relationship had to end, but I was hurting and needed my mom.

I was on my period and very emotional during the drive home, but I did all of the driving as usual. My mom told me what a trooper I was, and she couldn't believe how good of a driver I was. We had been on many road trips together but never this long. A few weeks prior I drove my car and my dog back to Arizona alone, so I didn't have to tow it since I'd never done that before.

We didn't have any weather issues on the trip home, and I was grateful. I didn't want to put my mom in any stressful situation, certainly not like any of the ones that I had been in in the past.

We got back to Arizona, put most of my things back in storage, and I moved in with my sister and her husband. I needed to save money for a while, before I would be able to get my own place again.

I started to work a lot more at PHX. My schedule got much better, and the money increased. We got a new contract, and our flight attendant hourly pay went up considerably. I still communicated with Marcus, occasionally during this time. And I noticed he was starting to grow up. He began to acknowledge the things that he had done to me, and acknowledge the things that I had done for him.

I didn't stay with my sister and her husband very long. They were also in a pretty toxic relationship, and it was stressful to be in their home.

Marcus was still on my benefits so he flew out to see me every once in a while, but the relationship was nothing more than "friends with benefits" as far as I was concerned.

I would never give my heart to him again, but this man became very attached to me during this time. He became grateful for the things that I had done for him. I could tell that he was actually in love with me for the first time. There were lots of ways that he tried to get me back. The trust was gone, and I couldn't take him back. I didn't love him.

He gave me the money for a deposit, so that I could get my own home and move out of my sister's home. He bought me nice things but nothing worked. I didn't trust him, and had zero respect for him, period.

I was happy to be moving into a nice apartment close to the airport. My son had been living with his father while I was gone, but now he could live with me again, and I was grateful for that.

May 2017
Losing M

During the time that I still lived with my sister, M, our dog, was getting old and had gotten very sick. He was almost fifteen and one day I just knew it was time to let him go, so I called my son, and told him that it was going to be M's last day, and that we needed to put him to sleep. M could barely walk, couldn't hold his bladder, and wasn't eating.

This was one of the hardest days of my life. I was grateful to have my family around me—my mom, my sister, and her husband, my son, and even one of my girlfriends came to say goodbye to M. He was such a special part of our family and my true soul connection. I was immediately lost without him. He protected me from Marcus on more than one occasion, when I lived with him back east.

I had his body cremated. I still have his ashes. He passed away on 30 May 2017, just a few months after I returned to Arizona. I think he was holding on for me, since he was all I had when I was living with Marcus back east. M must have known it was okay to pass away once I was safe back in Arizona with my family.

Not long after M died, I moved out of my sister's house September 2017, and to an apartment with my son.

It had only been a few months since M passed away, and my son's birthday was coming up. It was his twenty-third birthday, and he showed me a picture of this eight-week-old puppy, and that is what he wanted for his birthday. I couldn't say no, even though I was not over M passing away. I guess we both thought getting a new puppy would help.

This new dog was pure joy, and brought happiness to both of our lives. M passed on 30 May, and this new puppy per the breeder was born on 22 July. The moment I saw this puppy for the first time, I knew he was M's soul coming back to me and my family.

October 2018
New Home

I was flying a lot, loving my job and the routes that I was flying in Phoenix. Fortunately for me, about a year later in October of 2018, I had saved enough money that I could buy a home again.

Me, my son, and S our new dog moved into our new house in October 2018.

The money was getting better at work, and my schedule was also getting better. I started to be able to get some better days off and even an occasional holiday off. Life was good, and I was dating a little bit in Arizona.

Marcus was still around with simply a "friends with benefits" relationship, but he would come around if I needed him for whatever reason.

March 2019
Carl

In March of 2019, I met a man on the plane. We had to sit on the runway for a long time waiting for a gate at LAX, and he was sitting directly in front of my jump seat. We had a wonderful conversation. At the end of it when we finally arrived at the gate, and before he exited the plane, he asked for my phone number.

We immediately communicated with each other via text and on the phone several times a day. He lived in the LA area so I started bidding LAX layovers, so that I could see him. He was always coming to my hotel room, and I never thought much of it.

He asked me in the beginning what I was looking for in a man, and I was honest not recognizing his narcissistic behavior.

Since he asked, I told him everything—I told him ideally for me, and my job, I would be with someone who was self-employed, that the benefits of my job would help us travel, and I would work a lot less, and that I would be taken care of financially. That I was looking for a man that would be a true provider and protector, and that would allow my feminine energy to flow. Which is something that hadn't happened in any prior relationship.

I went deeper telling him about past relationships and my childhood.

I told him that I had a job since I was fourteen years old, and it was my turn to take a break, that I wanted to be taken care of, and in return I would be a good girlfriend, fiancée and/or wife. I'd be someone who is loyal, someone who could take care of a home and her man.

I didn't know it at the time, but when he asked me these questions it was just so that he could make himself appear to be exactly what I was looking for.

He told me he wanted to take care of me. He told me that he made a lot of money, he told me that he owned homes, he told me that he was self-employed, basically everything that I said I wanted. He created it.

I'd been in so many toxic relationships over the years that I truly wanted to believe in him. It took me two years to actually find out that the majority of it wasn't true, and that he was actually married.

Right before I met Carl, in February of 2019, the company put out a notice that they were going to be reducing our flight attendant base in Arizona.

I was devastated. I was finally doing well, no toxic man in my life, back in a home that I owned, and making money at a job that I loved.

I know that the main reason I allowed Carl in my life was because of the threat my company made, and my fear of having to work out of another city. Carl lived in the LA area, and we had a base in LA. That was in the back of my mind the day I met him, which was just one month after the company announced the possible displacements, so it was heavy on my mind, and that's probably why it took me so long to realize that he wasn't the man for me.

Nothing happened for a long time as far as being displaced out of Arizona, and then COVID happened in 2020.

March 2020
COVID

In March of 2020, COVID was affecting the entire United States. Many flight attendants were getting stuck in different cities and that included me. During this time, I never stopped working even though the company was offering leaves and was threatening to lay off people. I continued to work as usual, just with less people on my flights.

May 2020
Dad's Birthday

My father had been in a nursing home for many years. He started having health issues at the age of fifty-eight. He had a stroke at the age of sixty-two, and had been in a nursing home ever since with Senile Dementia.

His birthday this year was different, since we weren't able to go to his nursing home as a family to celebrate due to COVID. Our family had to wish him a happy birthday over FaceTime. The nursing home arranged it. We were having a celebration for him at my home with cake and food. My brothers, and my sister, my son, and my mom. We were all here celebrating his birthday, but we had to talk to him over FaceTime. It was very sad.

June 2020
Say Goodbye to Dad

Just a few days later, on 30 May, I received a voicemail from my father's nursing home that my father was coughing badly, and that they were going to test him for pneumonia. I was on a plane when the message was left, so I couldn't call the nursing home back right away.

Two days later on 2 June, at two a.m., I got a call from my father's nursing home again. This was odd for them to be calling at two a.m., so I knew that something was terribly wrong. The nurse said that my father was having a hard time breathing, and he wanted my permission to send him to the hospital.

There were so many things on the news at the time about hospitals and COVID, that I wasn't sure what to do. I told the nurse that I would call him right back, and I called my sister so that we could discuss it together. We were only on the phone a few minutes, and we decided to three-way call the nurse back. I asked the nurse to take the phone to my father, so that my father could hear my voice. I asked my father if he wanted to go to the hospital, and he simply said, "Yes."

That was the last word I heard my father speak.

I told the nurse immediately that he had my permission to send my father to the hospital. A few hours later, I received a phone call from the hospital. It was approximately five-thirty a.m. I spoke to the emergency room doctor. He told me that my father's oxygen level was zero and that he was being fully ventilated and on life support. I told the doctor that my father never wanted to be on life support and if that was the case, we were going to remove him from life support.

I knew there was a shortage of ventilators according to the news, so I wanted it to be used for someone who needed it, someone that would survive COVID.

I wanted to confirm this, so I asked the doctor if my father was removed from the ventilator, would he pass away, and he said "Yes." To me, that meant that the only reason my father was still alive was because of life support, which was a determining factor in removing him from life support.

The doctor explained to me the process and what was going to happen. I asked if my father was going to feel any pain, and he assured me that he would not. He explained the process, and he also explained that they were going to do a COVID test. He explained that if my father had COVID that no one would be able to enter the hospital, and that if he didn't have COVID only my sister and I, who were the medical power of attorneys, would be able to be in the room when he passed away.

The doctor told me that the COVID test would take several hours and he would be in contact with me later that day.

I got on the phone with my mom, my sister, and brothers, and decided that we should all just go to the hospital instead of waiting for the phone call.

We all arrived at the hospital at approximately eight a.m. It was me, my son, my two brothers, my sister, and my mom. We all walked into the main entrance of the hospital not knowing where my father was. The front desk told us that he was still in the emergency room. We walked into the emergency room together. There was someone standing behind a desk and two security guards. I knew that my father was still in the emergency room, and he was right on the other side of the door, yet they would not let us in, and they would not let me see my father. My family and I stood outside the hospital, not knowing what to do waiting for the phone to ring. Waiting for them to tell us if he had COVID, so that we would know how and when to remove his life support.

We decided to go to my sister's home to wait it out. Several hours later, the hospital called and said that my father was positive for COVID, and that we were not going to be able to be there with him to hold his hand to say goodbye. Losing my father was hard enough, but not being in the room to hold his hand while he passed was heartbreaking.

The nursing staff scheduled the time for us to do a FaceTime goodbye. The ICU nurse would be suited up, and she would call us when it was time. This is one of the most awful things I have ever experienced.

July 2020
Road Trip with Dad's Ashes

About a month after my father's funeral, I was in a very bad place. I knew that I was never going to be with Marcus again and I was dating Carl, who was emotionally and physically unavailable. I didn't know it at the time, but he was married.

I decided to get in my car with my dad's ashes in my t-shirt pocket and just drive. I figured I could get the clarity; I was searching for while I was on the road.

I started driving west not knowing where I was going. The week before, I had been on a layover in Denver. It was COVID time, and the only way I was able to get food was to have it delivered. I decided on Chinese food, and my fortune cookie said that I should travel to the nearest coast.

I was thinking about what that fortune said, when I got in my car that day. I started driving, and after being on the road for only about an hour traveling west on the I-10 my engine light came on. I figured it was something simple, like I didn't tighten my gas cap, and I would check it the next time I stopped.

Somewhere along the I-10, I decided to get off and travel northwest towards Lake Havasu. I don't know why I did this; it was just a feeling. I had to take that road. I stopped in Lake Havasu for a couple hours. I went to the lakeside, but knew that it wasn't where I was supposed to be. The fortune cookie said the coast nearest to me, which meant ocean, not a lake. I looked up the prices at the hotel rooms in Lake Havasu, and I just decided that wasn't where I was going to stop.

I continued to go north thinking maybe I would head towards Las Vegas, but when I reached I-40 I decided to continue west. My engine light was still on but the vehicle seemed to be okay, but I'd never driven on this part of the I-40 before. And didn't realize that I was going to be doing major climbing, and once I started the climb up the hill towards Barstow, I felt the engine pulling and missing.

The temperature wasn't rising on the car, but I thought for sure that I needed to stop for a while on the side of the road. I did that just to get my thoughts together, and to check the car the best I could.

I sat there for a while at an exit, before a highway patrol approached me. Even with nothing illegal in the car, a highway patrol approaching me for any reason was agonizing. It was very hot, and I had my windows down. I had some water so I was fine. He was kind. He just asked me if I was okay. I explained what was happening with the car. He told me that once I reach the top of the hill, it would be mostly downhill to Barstow, and that maybe I would be okay, that there were hotel rooms there etc. etc. I sat there for maybe thirty minutes or more, before I started to drive again.

I held my dad's ashes in my hand, and prayed that he would be there for me, and guide me, and get me somewhere safe. I ended up having to stop one more time before I reached Barstow, but I kept the ashes in my hand all the way up and down that hill. Somehow, I made it to Barstow where I found a repair shop that was closed, and a hotel room. I checked into the hotel and knew that I would have to spend the night there because the repair shop was closed until the morning.

I got settled in my hotel room and opened the window to my room and looked down. There was a Honda Goldwing just like what my dad had, when I was a kid. It was my sign that my dad was there with me, and that I would be okay.

The next morning, I was able to drive my car a mile down the road to a repair shop, but unfortunately all they were able to do was a diagnostic check. The Mechanic was kind enough to tell me that I should not let anyone in that town look at my Mercedes SUV. It seemed like it was a spark plug issue, and he didn't have the parts. He suggested that I have my vehicle towed to the nearest Mercedes dealership and there wasn't one in that town.

I had to check out of the hotel soon, so I started doing

research as to where the nearest Mercedes dealership was, and I found one in Ontario, California.

Ontario was about eighty miles away, but my roadside assistance was only going to cover towing for fifty miles, so I decided to try to at least drive the thirty miles and then call a tow truck. Fortunately for me, the road from Barstow to Ontario was mostly downhill, and I was able to make it all the way to the dealership, still holding on to dad's ashes.

When I was still in the hotel room, I sat my dad's ashes next to my credit card praying that it wasn't going to take a lot of money to fix whatever was wrong with my car.

I pulled into the Mercedes dealerships, and sat there for hours while they worked on my car. One of my spark plugs was bad, and it only cost about $300 to fix!

I still had no plan in place, but knew I didn't want to stay in Ontario, so I decided to head towards the coast just like the fortune cookie said.

I ended up at the Manhattan Beach Pier.

I had been in the car for a couple hours and needed to pee. I found a parking spot right in front of the beach bathrooms, and as I was walking to the bathroom, a beautiful monarch butterfly was buzzing around my head, something more like a bee instead of a butterfly. I knew instantly it was my father, that he was there with me. I went into the restroom, and when I walked back to my car the butterfly was still there. The butterfly landed at my feet and sat there flapping his wings for a really long time. I was talking to the butterfly and crying. People looked at me like I was crazy. The butterfly sat there so long that I was actually able to take a video of it that I still have in my phone today. I sat in my car and cried, but it felt more like a good cry. I felt close to my father, that I hadn't felt since I was a little girl, like somehow, he passed away and I got him back. His dementia was no longer there, and I had him back to be my guardian angel.

I decided to get a hotel room nearby, and spent a day or so in Manhattan Beach. I knew that I loved visiting the city, but somehow that day I felt a different connection to it like somehow that is where I was supposed to be, and the butterfly was surely that sign.

    I went back to Arizona a couple days later but was thinking about Manhattan Beach a lot.

August 2020
After Dad Died

I was still seeing Carl and still hadn't found out that he was married. He lived in Long Beach, but I had never been to his home. I found that strange and started to think about that a lot. I think this is when I started to realize that he was married, but I put it in the back of my mind and continued my relationship with him, but it certainly wasn't any kind of a commitment.

In August, that same year I met a pilot that I found very attractive. I was the lead flight attendant, and he was the captain on our flight from Minneapolis to Phoenix. My trip ended that day, but he had a three-hour sit in Phoenix before he would return to Dallas where he was based.

I never had any desire to date a pilot probably because most of them look like my father, but he was a beautiful fit black man. I'd never seen a pilot that looked like him. I was intrigued to say the least. He wasn't wearing a ring, so I assumed that he wasn't married. During a bathroom break when it was just him and I in the cockpit, we began flirting and he asked if he could walk me to my car during his break and before his next flight. I said yes, and we talked for a couple hours in the parking lot. He told me that he was married but he was separated, and the divorce papers were already filed.

I believed him or at least I wanted to. We began to communicate a lot. I saw him soon after that, and we dated a little bit over the next few months. We met each other on layovers, and it was great to be able to talk to him, and he understood my job.

I was still talking to Marcus occasionally and also to Carl, but I wasn't committed to anyone. As far as I was concerned, I was just dating three different men. All of them certainly had other women in their life, so I had zero expectations for any of them, and I was just having fun until I met my dream guy.

I know in my heart that being loyal, and being with one person is truly what I want. I thought that somehow with my dad's passing that he would direct me to the right man, to the person that I would grow old with.

When I first met the pilot, I thought it was him. I knew it wasn't Marcus. I knew it wasn't Carl, but maybe it was this man, my pilot, which would make perfect sense since lots of flight attendants marry pilots.

November 2020
Displacement

In November of 2020, it was official due to COVID that the Arizona FA base was going to be reduced, and at least eight hundred of us were going to either have to quit or move to another base.

I knew for sure; I wouldn't consider going back to the East Coast. That would be too close to Marcus, and I never wanted to live back there again.

I had a guy in LA, and I had a guy in Dallas, so I would try to get one of those bases, and have some familiarity and maybe end up with one of these guys.

I talked to my pilot guy about going to Dallas, but his divorce wasn't final, so he suggested that it wasn't the right time for me to come there. Go figure. He went on to say that he commuted for twenty years, and my best option would be to pick the closest city to PHX. I took his advice to choose LAX, but mostly because of my dad and the butterfly at Manhattan Beach. The feeling I got while I was there with the butterfly showed me that was where I was supposed to be. LAX was my number one choice and I got it. I figured I could work out of LAX and see Carl more, and even stay with him when I wasn't able to get a flight back home after a trip. Carl seemed to be excited about me coming to LAX. He said that he didn't want me to stay with him in Long Beach, since he was traveling full time for work, and it would be better if I had a place closer to the airport. He said that he would pay for me to have a crash pad while I look for an apartment near LAX, and that once I found an apartment he would sign the lease and pay the rent.

February 2021
New Base – LAX

I was officially based in LA. I was devastated at first, but I also remembered my road trip with my dad's ashes and how it led me to Manhattan Beach.

I was forced to be on reserve my first month in LA, so I would need to be there the whole month. I wouldn't have a schedule that would allow me to fly back home to PHX very often, so I packed what I could fit in my SUV, drove to LA, and I moved into a crash pad for $300 a month. I stayed there for three months while I looked for an apartment.

I was specifically looking for an apartment in areas that were only a few minutes away from LAX. I knew for a fact that I did not like LA traffic, and that I didn't ever want to be in a rush to get to work or stuck in traffic. I was looking at beach cities up and down the coast. Even though I knew, I was supposed to be in Manhattan beach, especially since it was the closest beach city to LAX. I looked in Redondo Beach, Hermosa Beach, and of course Manhattan Beach.

Carl told me that he would pay for the apartment, and that he would do the application, and pay for the deposit. I found a few places that I liked, but it seemed like every time I found a place he never did the application fast enough, and I lost out on a couple places. It was starting to feel a little fishy to me, but I really needed to get out of the crash pad. I was forty-eight years old climbing into a bunk bed, and sharing a room with five other women.

May 2021
Manhattan Beach Apartment

I knew I really needed a place, since commuting back home was going to be a nightmare. One hundred and twenty-five FAs got sent to LAX, so there was a lot of competition for the jump seats. Flights from LAX were always full, and my airline only had a few flights per day. I needed help from Carl getting a place in LAX, since I still owned my home in Phoenix. I couldn't afford both places, but didn't want to sell my house in AZ.

Since Carl was being flakey, I decided to reach out to Marcus. I knew Marcus had some business in the LA area so I contacted him and asked him if he was going to be doing any work in LA, and if he wanted to consider getting an apartment with me to share. No strings attached. He said yes, but this really wasn't what I wanted, since I figured he would use this opportunity to try to get back together with me, and I truly didn't want that.

At this point, we still had a "friends with benefits" relationship, but I knew he wanted more so he would do anything for me. I should have felt guilty for using him as a backup plan but I didn't.

He was just a backup plan in case Carl didn't follow through.

After looking at about fifty apartments, I found the perfect place and I wasn't willing to lose this place waiting on Carl, so I did the application on my own.

I knew that if I needed money, Marcus would give it to me. To this day, I think he feels an obligation to me for the things I did for him, and that's really why I didn't feel guilty.

I wanted this place. I knew it was the one. I had to have an in-person interview with the landlord. I went to the landlord's home just a few miles away from the apartment and did the application there. He interviewed me like I was applying for a job. We instantly hit it off, especially when I told him about my father and the butterfly at the Manhattan beach pier. He had three hundred plus people apply for this apartment, and he picked me. It was meant to be and I was approved on my own, just me on the lease!

Everything was falling into place. I loved being based in LA, since my schedule was much better, and now I had the perfect apartment one block from the beach and five mins to my parking spot at LAX.

This apartment required a large deposit and the first month's rent which was $5000 total. Carl gave me the entire amount, but I did the application alone so he wasn't on the lease, and I know now he had no intention of moving in with me.

Carl was working in San Francisco full time and living in a hotel. I went to visit him there a couple times a month, but he never came to LA to stay with me at the apartment he was paying for. After about an additional year of casually dating him, I became uncomfortable with the situation. I wanted and needed more from him, and I didn't understand why that wasn't happening.

April 2022
Carl's Background Check

I flew to San Francisco to see Carl for his birthday. Something felt off kinda, like it always had from the very beginning.

I decided I just didn't want to be in this relationship anymore, so I needed to find my way out. When I got back home from spending his birthday with him, I decided to do a background check on him.

The address that he told me he lived at in Long Beach wasn't showing up as a home he owned or even rented currently. It did show up as a past address. The address that did show up for him as his current address was in Texas, which was odd to me as he told me he still lived in Long Beach. The address in Texas also showed a female's name as a close relative, and that was my absolute indication that he was married.

I confronted him with what I found, and sent him pictures of what I found on the site. But he continued to say that he was not married, and that he lived in Long Beach.

I told him that our relationship was over, but he begged me not to break up with him whatever that meant and that he was still going to be paying the rent. I don't know why he would do that when I refused to see him anymore, but he did continue to pay.

April 2022
Done with Men from the Past

In April of 2022, after I did the background check on Carl, I decided that I should start dating in LA. Manhattan Beach is where I was supposed to be because of my dad, the butterfly, my job, etc. It was time to be done with any man from the past.

I spent that summer flying a lot, and really just focusing on me enjoying my time alone at the beach and on my layovers.

I got on Tinder and started dating in LA. I went on a couple of good dates, and I went on several awful dates, but all just really for fun not looking for anything serious.

I was going to be turning fifty in November of 2022, and I started planning my birthday party with my girlfriends, a few months in advance that same summer. I knew that I didn't want to spend my fiftieth birthday alone, and without a date. I started thinking about which one of the men from my past I would allow to spend my birthday with me, if any since I was supposed to be done with all of them.

I couldn't really make that decision at first. I didn't want any of them but wanted to have a dance partner who wasn't a stranger.

I met a couple different men on the flights over the last year. I was just casually dating nothing serious, certainly not anyone that I would consider being my date for my fiftieth birthday.

The month prior to my birthday is when I began this book, the same time that I was talking to Lamar, my Hollywood friend, that I met on the plane.

I also went on another road trip that October with my son to Mexico.

October 2022
Road Trip with My Son

The story about my life was heavy on my mind because of the communication that I was having with my Hollywood friend about writing this story. I was thinking about it a lot on the way to Mexico with my son.

My son had heard me talking about being arrested a couple times, and I wasn't really trying to hide it from him anymore, but we never actually had a conversation about it.

On our way to Mexico, and after we crossed the border into Mexico, we were pulled over by the local police. I've never been in a car with my son, a black man, and gotten pulled over. Every officer related shooting of a black man was circling in my head. My son was driving, and everything that I ever experienced being pulled over including the time with my boyfriend when he was hogtied on the side of the road was running through my mind.

My heart was pounding out of my chest, and once again I found a way to compose myself. We didn't have anything illegal in the car, but we were in another country and didn't speak the language, so I figured this would not be good.

The opposite happened. The officers laughed and talked with us. They liked my son's black curly hair and thought he was someone famous. The perception that every young fit black male is an athlete is presumed in Mexico just like the US, go figure.

We were pulled over in a speed trap, through which the police would shake down Americans for bribe money. We didn't end up paying them anything, and they let us go apparently because they thought my son was a famous athlete.

The panic that I felt before they let us go, led me to realizing this was the perfect opportunity to tell my son everything.

During the rest of the hour's drive to the beach we were

headed to, I told him about everything that I've written in this story. He couldn't believe it. He told me I had to write a book. He told me I needed to make a movie and because that was right around the same time that I was talking to Lamar, and he encouraged me to start writing. I knew that it was going to happen soon.

October 2022
The Writing Began

I started writing that same month still not knowing the ending of this story and remembering what my Hollywood friend told me about not needing an ending to begin.

My fiftieth birthday was right around the corner and planning it took a lot of time and energy, so after the first time I started writing this story in October of 2022, I put it aside until the beginning of 2023, after I was already fifty and when the holidays were over.

Right before my fiftieth birthday party and still not knowing who my date was going to be, I had a long layover on the East Coast. Marcus still lived back east, and I asked him to come and join me on my layover so I could tell him in person that I had officially started writing a book. We had a wonderful night. We went dancing, which is the only place that I've ever felt loved by this man, so it made sense we would have a good night. We did. We went salsa dancing and danced for hours. He agreed and encouraged me to continue writing, although he must have assumed that I wouldn't tell the whole truth about him. We had such a great night, and my birthday was right around the corner, so I decided to ask him to be my date.

My fiftieth birthday was going to be a night of dancing in AZ. I knew that I would have a great time with Marcus, so I officially asked him to be my date. He said yes.

My birthday was wonderful. I had such a great time with my girlfriends, my son, my family, and even Marcus. I knew I still didn't want to be with this man. He was still on my flight benefits, so it was easy for him to fly in and join me for my birthday, then fly right back out the next day with no strings attached.

19 November, 2022
My Happy Ending!

A few weeks before my birthday, I noticed that a guy I was friends with on FB kept liking some of my posts. I knew who this man was. I had a crush on him for many years.

I remember seeing him out at some of the clubs I used to go to with Marcus and my girlfriends. I remember how beautiful I thought his smile was. I didn't pay that much attention to his "likes" on my post until they started to be consistent. I figured that eventually he would message me, and maybe ask me out but that didn't happen.

I liked his posts as well, but his posts weren't ever anything very personal. I could tell that he was a football fan and which team he followed. I looked at my team's schedule and noticed that our teams were going to play each other soon, so I messaged him on Facebook and asked him if he wanted to watch that game together.

He said, "Yes." At this point, I didn't even know if this was a real Facebook page or if it was really him, but I thought why not.

We messaged back and forth a couple times and started to plan the date, but that was a few weeks away and I wanted to meet him before that.

Being based in LA, I was now able to have layovers in AZ. I would sometimes go to my home on these layovers, and sometimes I would stay at the hotel, and have my sister or girlfriends come stay, and go out with me for dinner or drinks or dancing.

I was scheduled to have a layover at home on 19 November. It was a long layover on a Friday night at a great hotel.

Instead of waiting to watch a football game together, I

decided to ask him if he wanted to join me at my hotel in downtown Phoenix for a drink, since he lived in Arizona.

That day, I was scheduled to work a flight from LA to Cabo and then from Cabo to Phoenix. I told him that I was going to arrive at my hotel about eight p.m., and he said he would meet me at the bar. When I arrived at the hotel, he was not there yet, so I went up to my room, made myself a drink, and freshened up. At some point, he told me that he was sitting at the bar and that I could come down to meet him. Still at that point, I didn't know if it was really him, and I was very nervous. I thought I was possibly being "catfished."

To my delight, it was really him. The moment I saw his beautiful familiar smile, that I had a crush on for so many years, I was no longer nervous. Then his embrace was comfortable and soothing, especially since I had just worked two flights that day. I immediately started thinking how nice it would be to have a hug like that after work.

He sat back down and I joined him. He already had a drink while he was waiting for me, and I had already had one in the room, so we were both feeling good. I ordered another drink. We ordered some food, and the conversation flowed like we had known each other forever.

I asked the normal first-date questions. He knew I was a flight attendant from my post, but since his posts weren't personal, I didn't know what he did for a living.

He told me he was a TRUCK DRIVER and owned a trucking business!

I'm not sure if he could tell the joy that my heart felt in that moment. My whole life flashed before me at that moment. I felt like I was eight years old again, climbing up into my uncle and aunt's semi-truck.

My connection to him was immediate and ironic.

My life had come full circle at this moment. I prayed to myself while sitting across from him. Please let this man be my happy ending…

The End

Epilogue

Call me foolish, call me crazy, but when you know, you know. I fell in love with my truck driver that first night.

I knew immediately that he was my person, my soulmate, my one, true love of a lifetime. The date with him was not only my best "first" date of my life but one of the best nights of my life, period.

We sat at the hotel bar for a couple hours. Everything we talked about we had in common. The conversation flowed with ease, each other taking turns to listen. We connected and the chemistry was wonderful, even overwhelming. We said things like "where have you been all my life."

I've had good first dates in the past, but, somehow, this was so very different.

We drank and shared a plate of chicken nachos. He fed me chips from his hand and wiped a spot of cheese from my chin. When he did that, it was the second time he touched me. The first time was the hug when we first approached each other. Even then with that first hug, that first touch, I knew I wanted him to keep touching me forever. We ate and drank together like we had been lovers for years.

After a couple hours of talking and drinking and having a great time, I needed to use the restroom. I asked him to join me in my hotel room, instead of using the lobby restroom. There was no point in making this man wait. I wanted him, and it was clear he wanted me also, so up to my room we went.

The first kiss was amazing. His lips were soft and his tongue made me melt. After standing near the window looking out over the city and kissing, he took my hand and led me to the bed. He started removing my blouse, then my bra. He looked at me and my breast like they were the prettiest things he had ever seen.

Then he sat me down on the bed and removed the four-inch heels that I wore to look sexy for him on our date.

Once he removed my heels, he caressed my feet and began kissing them while he was staring up at me. Our eye contact was piercing. Next, he removed my jeans and panties.

When he slid them off, the wetness in my panties must have been noticeable, since he said how beautiful my wet pussy looked. Then he was playing with my clit and entering me with his fingers.

He was still fully dressed as I was lying on the bed, but I was completely naked. Watching him undress felt like forever, and I couldn't wait to have him inside of me. He took his time removing everything, and I could tell he liked me watching him as he slowly removed everything. Our eye contact continued while he removed his clothes, and I felt like we were one even before he was inside of me. He stood there with his hard cock in his hand, letting me watch for a few seconds before he joined me on the bed.

He kissed and caressed my breast. He took his kisses, his tongue, and his fingers to my pussy. He licked me where no one ever had before. He took his time, and since all of this felt so good, I took my time letting him please me.

I don't know how long his face was between my legs, but it felt like hours and once I reached orgasm, he came back to my face and kissed me over and over, before he finally entered me with his hard cock.

We made love for hours. First, he took me with him on top. Somehow, he instinctively knew that's how I would cum again. Then, he took me from behind. Not rough, but not gentle either. Just enough to fill me up and make me feel dominated for a few minutes. Then, finally, he lay on his back and let me ride him, until he, himself, reached orgasm.

We lay together for a few minutes, before he got up and got dressed. I stayed in the bed with his cum inside of me, since we never even discussed using a condom. After he was dressed and was ready to leave, he said to me that he had a vasectomy, so I didn't need to worry about getting pregnant. I simply said okay.

I had zero expectations. The intimacy of our lovemaking was mesmerizing and wonderful. I wasn't sure if I would ever hear from him again, and I didn't care at that moment.

He apparently had a wonderful time that night as well and we started communicating, often having dates once or twice a week whenever I was in Arizona. The relationship developed so much that I knew that he was my person.

He had everything that I was looking for in a lifetime partner. He was self-employed and made a lot of money. He loved to watch sports, camp, travel, fish, drive fast cars and motorcycles. All these things reminded me of my dad. He even looked like a black version of Dad. Not tall but not short, sexy strong arms, and a beautiful smile. A little round in the stomach, bald and bearded just like my dad.

He made me feel special, loved, and safe. I trusted him. I gave him my heart, my soul, and my everything. I had zero insecurities when I was with him. He looked at me and made me feel as though I was the only woman in the world.

I couldn't wait to start doing the things with my truck driver that I did with my dad, when I was a child and young adult.

The adventures with my dad ended after he had a stroke, and the results of the stroke led to dementia. After the stroke, he had to be placed in a nursing home. He was no longer able to do the things he loved to do with me and his family. I'd missed those times enough to know they were an important part of my life, and I wanted to be with a man who enjoyed those same hobbies.

But there was one thing I wanted to do with my truck driver more than any other, and that was ride in his semi-truck, but that didn't happen for a couple months...

I joined him on a trip when he was taking a load from Nashville, TN, to Houston, TX. It was the best three days of my life. Being in the truck made me feel at home. Watching him drive that truck made me feel safe. While I was looking at him driving the truck, I saw the sexiest man alive. There was no doubt...

He was my person.